The Green Roof Manual

The Green Roof Manual

A Professional Guide to Design, Installation, and Maintenance

Edmund C. Snodgrass and Linda McIntyre

Timber Press
Portland ▪ London

Frontispiece: This extensive green roof at Penn State University
uses a few perennials and grasses to increase the ornamental value.

Published in 2010 by Timber Press, Inc.

The Haseltine Building
133 S.W. Second Avenue, Suite 450
Portland, Oregon 97204-3527
www.timberpress.com

2 The Quadrant
135 Salusbury Road
London NW6 6RJ
www.timberpress.co.uk

Printed in China

Library of Congress Cataloging-in-Publication Data
Snodgrass, Edmund C.
    The green roof manual : a professional guide to design, installation, and
maintenance/ Edmund C. Snodgrass and Linda McIntyre.
        p. cm.
    Includes bibliographical references and index.
    ISBN 978-1-60469-049-1
    1. Roof gardening. I. McIntyre, Linda, 1964– II. Title.
    SB419.5.S65 2010
    635.9'671dc22
                                                        2010005074
A catalog record for this book is also available from the British Library.

Contents

Campanulas light up a green roof on a dormitory at Swarthmore College outside Philadelphia.

Acknowledgments

This book would not have been possible without the generous help of all the people who have given time and support solely to advance green roof technology. Penn State University, Michigan State University, Oregon State University, The University of Maryland, The University of Auckland, The California Academy of Sciences, The Lady Bird Johnson Wildflower Center, and the cities of Portland, Oregon, and Chicago have all shared their research and their time and opened their facilities for photographic visits. The American Society of Landscape Architects headquarters, the Library of Congress' National Audio Video Conservation Center, Swarthmore College, and Dansko gave me an open invitation to show up any time with my camera. Many thanks to all the people—too numerous to mention individually—from all corners of the industry who shared their insights and gave us feedback.

Thanks to the crew at Emory Knoll Farms who supported my time away and who are the most fabulous folks to work alongside. Big thanks to my wife, Lucie, who supports me always without fail.

Most of all, this book would not have been written without my coauthor, Linda McIntyre, who has put in countless hours writing, interviewing, and sweating all the details to produce what we hope will be a book of value.

—ED SNODGRASS

Writing this book was a truly collaborative process—not just between Ed and me, but among us and a slew of generous and patient experts. Properly thanking everyone who deserves it would require an additional book, but I'm obliged to give a special shout-out to a few of these experts. Charlie Miller of Roofscapes has been the go-to engineer for this English major since my first acquaintance with green roofs as a staff writer and editor at *Landscape Architecture* magazine. While I have not had the opportunity to take his classes, I know from experience that Rob

Berghage of Penn State University's Center for Green Roof Research is a great teacher. Peter Philippi and Jörg Breuning of Green Roof Service unstintingly shared the expertise they developed on both sides of the Atlantic. All of these busy people withstood my incessant questioning with good grace and provided the substance that fills these pages.

Bill Thompson, my former boss and the steward of *Landscape Architecture* until autumn 2009, encouraged me to pursue my interest in green roofs, demanded critical analysis rather than superficial cheerleading, and impressed on me the importance of providing readers with useful, accessible, and well-organized information. His comments and suggestions, as well as those lessons, improved this book immensely.

I would also like to acknowledge the help of the following individuals, whom graciously shared insights from the field: Jason Abbey, Associate, FXFOWLE Architects; Glen Abrams, Philadelphia Water Department, Office of Watersheds; Paul Bassett, founder of Hydro-Logix Solutions, Inc.; Ed Beaulieu, Chief Sustainability Officer, Aquascape, Inc.; Michael Berkshire, Green Projects Administrator, City of Chicago; Jeffrey Bruce, President, Jeffrey L. Bruce & Company, Landscape Architects and Planners; Jim Burton, Construction Services; Stephen Bushnell, Product Director, Fireman's Fund Insurance Company; Ayehlet Cooper, Horticulturist, Furbish Company; Patrick Cullina, Vice President of Horticulture and Facilities, Brooklyn Botanic Garden; Lance Davis, Sustainable Design Expert, U.S. General Services Administration; Darren DeStefano, Horticulturist, U.S. General Services Administration; Laura Dickinson, graduate student, Columbia University; Angie Duhrman, Green Roof Manager, Tecta America Corporation; Michael Furbish, President, Furbish Company; Stuart Gaffin, Associate Research Scientist, Center for Climate Systems Research, Columbia University; Drew Gangnes, Director of Civil Engineering, Magnusson Klemencic Associates; Mark Gaulin, Senior Vice President and Chief Operating Officer, Tecta America, and founder of Magco; Dusty Gedge, wildlife consultant and cofounder of livingroofs.org; Robert Goo, Environmental Protection Specialist, U.S. Environmental Protection Agency; Alan Good, Landscape Exhibits Supervisor, California Academy of Sciences; Chris and Lisa Goode, owners of Goode Green green roof design and installation; Denis Gray, owner of Denis Gray Horticulture; Ken Hercenberg, Associate Vice President and Specifications Leader, Cannon Design; Elizabeth Kennedy, Elizabeth Kennedy Landscape Architects; Nancy Kiefer, Director of Facilities and Office Services, World Resources Institute; Jason King, Landscape Architect, Greenworks; Peter Kjellerup, founder of Dansko; Chris Kloss, Senior Environmental Scientist, Low Impact Development Center; Michael Krawiec, Project Manager, URS Corporation; Tom Liptan, Portland Bureau of Environmental Services; John Loomis, SWA Group; David MacKenzie, owner of LiveRoof LLC; Hanna Packer, Design Associate, Town and Gardens Ltd.; Matt Palmer, Department of Ecology, Evolution, and Environmental Biology, Columbia University; Daria Payne, Facilities Manager, Dansko; Greg Raymond, Managing Member, Ecogardens; Steve Sawyer, Plant Manager, Sidwell Friends School; Mike Saxenian, Assistant Head of School and Chief Financial Officer, Sidwell Friends School; Mark Simmons, Ecologist, Lady Bird Johnson Wildflower Center; Jennifer W. Souder, Assistant Director and Director of Capital Projects, Queens Botanical Garden; Jim Stamer, President, Prospect Waterproofing Company; Jeanette Stewart, founder and President, Lands and Waters; Brian Taylor, Civil Design Engineer, Magnusson Klemencic Associates; Dennis Wilde, Principal, Gerding Edlen Development; Mary Wyatt, Executive Director, TKF Foundation; and Jennifer Zuri, Marketing Communications Manager, Aquascape, Inc.

My coauthor's vast knowledge and experience, and his calm in the face of my own flappability, made the difficult task of wrestling this book into shape not only possible but fun. I'll miss the regular sessions with the crew at Emory Knoll Farms (and the frequent ice cream breaks at Broom's Bloom dairy, just up the road). Ed and I also want to thank Tom Fischer and the rest of the team at Timber Press and our excellent editor, Lisa DiDonato Brousseau, for their guidance, support, and expertise.

Finally, I could not have finished this project without my husband, Jeff, whose love, support, patience, kindness, and dinners sustained me throughout the process.

—Linda McIntyre

Green roofs are increasingly popular on college campuses. This dormitory at Swarthmore College has green roofs on two levels, one of which is visible from inside the building.

Introduction

In their 2006 book *Green Roof Plants*, Ed and Lucie Snodgrass provided North American readers with the first comprehensive guide to selecting and planting species that can survive on a rooftop, and in doing so introduced many readers to the concept of green roofs. Though only a few years have passed since that book was written, it seems appropriate now, as green building enters the mainstream and economic trends force a reassessment of priorities, to take a broader view, going beyond green roof horticulture and looking at how far the industry has come since the first extensive green roofs were built in North America a little over a decade ago. We wrote this book for a wide audience including everyone who might be involved with a green roof project: the client, architect, landscape architect, roofing contractor, ecologist, nurseryman, property manager, and maintenance team.

More green roofs in more places have added breadth as well as depth to what we know about how this technology, mature in Europe but less tested in our more variable climate and more freewheeling regulatory and building cultures, performs in North America. While it's still early in the life of North America's green roof industry, the performance of those roofs over time has to some extent clarified the trade-offs among different approaches and underscores the importance of maintenance. And as more projects are built, the obstacles encountered by industry pioneers, and their successes, can inform the choices made by those who follow.

The pool of information available to people interested in the topic or considering green roofs for their projects is expanding rapidly. A lot of this information, however, has been published only in government reports or scientific journals such as *HortScience*, and much of it is anecdotal, held by people too busy designing and building green roofs to write articles or books. Some of the information available in the general-interest media or online is misleading or applicable only in a particular region or in narrow circumstances. Our goal was to harvest the most pertinent lessons from the field and its leaders and to make those lessons accessible to both casual and serious readers.

In addition to assessing the conventional wisdom, we have put it to the test by asking designers, builders, scientists, and the people who live and work under green roofs what they have learned from those projects. We have talked with experts in every aspect of the industry to find answers to questions we hear again and again: How do you design and build a green roof that will last without extraordinary intervention over the long term? What are the most common factors in unsuccessful projects? Which parts of North America are best suited to green roofs? Are there places where green roofs are unlikely to thrive in any

High-profile projects such as Millennium Park in Chicago have generated interest in green roofs.

circumstances? How can designers and builders make sure that clients are prepared for the aesthetics of a just-planted green roof, and that they understand the commitment involved over time to ensure a green roof's success? What is the relationship between a green roof and the surrounding landscape at grade? Can native plants thrive on a green roof? Is it possible for a green roof environment to accommodate herbs, fruits, and vegetables?

We have visited green roofs throughout North America and around the world, taking note of which approaches have been most successful and which design objectives have been consistently difficult to achieve and maintain. We have discussed with designers and builders how to integrate a green roof into a project, at both the building and the site scales, and how to most

Green roofs are well established in some European countries, such as Switzerland.

effectively integrate green roofs with other measures to mitigate a building's impact on the landscape. We have asked scientists about the extent to which research and monitoring have confirmed and quantified the benefits of green roof technology. We have asked clients whether their expectations have been met or exceeded. We have asked the staff maintaining green roofs—when there is such a staff—what their greatest challenges are, how they solve common problems, and how they keep those roofs healthy and thriving.

Our intention is to help people navigate the green roof design, installation, and maintenance processes, not to provide all of the answers. If there is one thing we have learned during the process of writing this book, it is that there are few certainties in the world of green roofs. A green roof takes a form for which there are hundreds, even thousands, of variables—a building—and imposes on it a form even more fluid—a living landscape. The appearance of a successful project will change over time, and its performance might vary with climatic changes. Green roof design and installation is, to some degree, a leap of faith. But a growing number of people believe the result is worthwhile, whether the desired outcome is less sewage discharged into local rivers and streams, a softening of the urban hardscape, or simply a garden in the sky.

We've presented our findings in a way that we hope will be useful to readers with varying needs. A brief discussion of green roof benefits and components comes first. An update on the industry and incentives being put in place by more and more local governments also comes early in the book. Keeping up with the rapidly changing regulatory landscape is challenging—it will have changed even since this book went to print—but some trends are apparent. For example, stormwater management infrastructure is overburdened in many cities, and green roofs are one way to take some of the pressure off by mitigating runoff into those systems. Cities are experimenting with innovative ways to encourage the private sector to go green, including tax incentives, density bonuses, and green-space requirements. What are the early results of these programs?

We also discuss how to put together your green roof project team. This is a truly interdisciplinary technology—in effect a system engineered to live and breathe, comprising architecture, engineering, horticulture, and ecology, as well as other disciplines depending on the scope and objectives of the project. While a weekend hobbyist might want to build a green roof on his or her garage to see what happens, most people will not want to use a green roof project as an opportunity for experimentation.

Those who have already decided to use a green roof in their own projects can, if they wish, go directly to chapters 4 and 5 to examine different design paradigms including examples of each and lessons to take away. A lot of green roof construction has been and will continue to be driven by stormwater regulations, but those who want a greater emphasis on aesthetics have options, too. Anyone considering a green roof, simple or elaborate, would be well served by firming up their objectives as early as possible in the process. To help them along, we examine the pros and cons of each approach.

Even the merely curious reader should make sure to read the chapter on maintenance, which often makes the difference be-

Maintenance keeps a green roof healthy and attractive.

tween a thriving green roof and a failed one. As an unusual hybrid of engineering and ecology, a green roof has a particular set of needs, which can in many cases be met with regular observation and limited intervention. Despite the promises one sometimes encounters in the field, green roofs are not maintenance-free, and people define "low maintenance" in very different ways. Those who hesitate to commit adequate resources to this unexciting but critical function might want to reconsider whether a green roof is right for their project.

Readers in search of more information can find our suggestions in the Resources section. We've gathered sources, most available online, for general and industry information, policy and incentives, academic research programs, certification and accreditation, and other helpful references.

Why aren't all new roofs green?

These days you can find a lot of literature rhapsodizing about how wonderful and environmentally friendly green roofs are and how sustainable design can save the planet and even the distressed economy. But it will take more than high hopes and feel-good slogans to bring about the widespread adoption of green roof technology and other complementary sustainable building practices.

That will take a frank discussion of the challenges, commitment, and costs involved as well as the benefits. It will require clients and designers to make choices and trade-offs. It will involve the collection and dissemination of data that show that, from a life-cycle accounting standpoint, green roofs and other low-impact designs are less expensive and more efficient that pipes and detention basins, even though they might cost more at the outset. It will require research into the nitty-gritty of construction and the sometimes difficult, but usually necessary, work of maintenance and a clear-eyed appraisal about what works and what does not. We hope this book will make a modest but meaningful contribution to this process.

Intensive green roofs have deep soil that can support trees, shrubs, and lots of visitors.

1 Green Roof Basics

Key Points

- A green roof is not a typical roof garden.
- Potential benefits include:
    - stormwater management
    - longer life for the roof membrane
    - reduction in energy costs
    - mitigation of the urban heat island effect (if widely implemented)
    - habitat for urban wildlife
    - amenity value, aesthetics, and marketing appeal.
- Green roofs are relatively new in North America but popular and proven in Europe.

What is a green roof?

Green roofs, also known as eco-roofs, living roofs, planted roofs, or vegetated roofs, use plants to improve a roof's performance, its appearance, or both. Green roofs are often described as falling into one of two categories: intensive and extensive.

There are no technical definitions of these terms, but as generally understood intensive green roofs are more like conventional roof gardens. They have deeper, more organic growing medium or soil capable of supporting a wide variety of plants, often including shrubs and small trees. They are usually accessible for regular use and often designed as amenities for people who live or work in the building.

Extensive green roofs are simpler, lighter, and thinner in profile. They usually have a depth of about 6 inches (15 cm) or less of coarse, mineral-based growing medium and are usually planted primarily with sedums and other tough, drought-resistant, low-growing plants, though more colorful accent plants might be mixed in. This kind of green roof is a popular ecological building tool in Europe. In Germany, where green roofs are plentiful, more than 80 percent of them are extensive (Philippi 2006).

This book focuses largely on the latter category because we believe that extensive green roofs produce the greatest return on investment in both economic and ecological terms—they are, or

Green roofs adorn all kinds of buildings in Europe.

Extensive green roofs, especially when installed on a wide scale, provide a range of benefits including stormwater management.

should be, easier and less expensive to design and build. If built on a large scale in cities, they show promise for significant energy savings and other environmental benefits as well as a less tangible improvement in the quality of urban life. Furthermore, there are few practical resources available for those seeking information about designing, building, and maintaining extensive green roofs outside of Europe and adapting the technology to different climates. Readers interested in more complex roof gardens might find some of the information in this book of use, but for more detailed information they should consult one of the books on that subject that have stood the test of time, such as *Planting Green Roofs and Living Walls* by Nigel Dunnett and Noel Kingsbury (2008, Timber Press) and *Roof Gardens: History, Design, Construction* (1999, W. W. Norton) by Theodore Osmondson.

Green roof benefits

While even the most basic extensive green roofs usually look better than their tar- or asphalt-clad conventional counterparts, they are most often built for reasons other than aesthetics. Green roof benefits have been well documented in Europe. A growing body of data from North America, Asia, and Australia suggests

Flat black roofs are ugly, hot, dirty, and often short-lived.

that, with a carefully considered design intent, a design adjusted for both the regional climate and the roof's microclimates, proper installation, and a maintenance program to ensure long-term viability, they can work equally well in other places. Green roofs make more sense, of course, in some climates than in others (desert areas, for example, might present special challenges).

But more research is needed, in part to overcome resistance based on fear or lack of knowledge. A lot of the existing data come from small test plots in controlled situations, not large green roofs on buildings whose performance over time has been measured and analyzed. The efforts underway represent a good start, but validated performance in the field is what will make or break green roofs as a tool in the sustainable construction arsenal.

It's difficult to make a lot of generalizations about green roofs because the actual benefits provided on a particular site depend on many variables. Climate conditions in North America are much more heterogeneous than in western Europe. Few standards for design details and materials exist here, and most projects are not monitored, so data are scant and reliable prediction of performance is difficult.

A green roof can be designed to maximize one kind of benefit, but that improved performance might come at the cost of another or make the project significantly more complex and ex-

Green roofs are easily installed on many flat-roofed buildings. Even simple designs are attractive as well as functional.

pensive. While some individual projects do provide some benefits to the building owner and its residents or employees, others, such as reduction of the urban heat island effect, can only be maximized if the approach is implemented on a broad scale. However well intentioned or unintentional it is, the overselling of potential benefits by uncritical advocates will only undermine the reputation of green roofs in the marketplace over the long term.

Keeping those caveats in mind, it's becoming clearer that green roofs *can* be good tools to achieve many ecological objectives. Potential benefits include stormwater management; longer life for the roof membrane; lower energy costs; mitigation of the urban heat island effect; habitat for urban wildlife; and amenity value, aesthetics, and marketing.

Stormwater management

Stormwater runoff carries pollutants. When it rains, water running off conventional roofs and paved areas picks up and carries deposited pollutants to rivers, streams, and other local bodies of water. Contaminants in stormwater runoff can include fertilizers, herbicides, and insecticides from both farms and residential developments; oil and grease from roads and energy production facilities; sediment from construction sites, farmland, and stream banks; salts and acid drainage from farmland and abandoned mines; and nutrients and bacteria from farm animals, pet waste, and malfunctioning septic systems (U.S. Environmental Protection Agency [EPA] 1994). In the United States alone, more than 10 trillion gallons (38 trillion L) of this untreated runoff flow into receiving waters every year (EPA 2004a). The resulting contamination harms aquatic life, reducing the diversity of insect and fish populations (Center for Watershed Protection 2003). It can also make water unsafe for humans: Stormwater runoff is the greatest contributor to beach closings and advisories based on unsafe levels of bacteria (Natural Resources Defense Council 2008).

Runoff interferes with natural hydrology. The increased quantity of runoff during storms, and the rate at which that water is discharged from sewer systems into rivers and streams, also cause problems including floods, increased sediment loads, and erosion of stream banks. The increased flow from smaller, frequently oc-

Combined sewer overflows send stormwater mixed with pollutants, including raw sewage, into receiving waters.

curring storms is of particular concern because it has not been effectively addressed by regulation or traditional stormwater management measures aimed only at large, infrequent storms (Pitt 1999; National Research Council 2008). In addition, stormwater runoff during hot summer months contributes to higher temperatures in rivers and streams—temperatures can rise as much as 5 to 12°F (3 to 7°C)—potentially compromising the health of temperature-sensitive aquatic species (EPA 2004b).

Stormwater runoff impairs water quality and increases the quantity, velocity, and temperature of water running through rivers and streams. Photograph by Linda McIntyre

The increased flow through rivers and streams after storms can erode and destabilize banks. Photograph by Linda McIntyre

Land development produces runoff. Before land is developed, natural systems accommodate stormwater and runoff is not a problem. Leaves and undisturbed soil absorb rain, sustain plant life, and recharge groundwater levels. Rough and uneven topography, plants, and other features of the unbuilt landscape slow the flow of water running over its surface into rivers, streams, lakes, and ponds. Less fertile areas with fewer plants have their own adaptations to handle stormwater. But as more and more remote suburban and rural areas are developed, with attendant increases in pavement, buildings, and other impervious surfaces, runoff volume increases dramatically, and managing it becomes more urgent.

Land has been developed at an aggressive pace in recent years. From 1997 until 2001, rural land in the United States was developed at an average rate of 6000 acres (2400 ha) every day (National Resources Conservation Service 2003). A 2004 study by the National Oceanic and Atmospheric Administration's National Geophysical Data Center estimated that the impervious surface area of the contiguous United States was roughly the size of Ohio, and slightly larger than the area covered by herbaceous wetlands (Elvidge et al. 2004). Without porous surfaces through which it can filter through soil and recharge groundwater, storm-

Stormwater runoff has little impact on less developed land. It infiltrates uncompacted soil or travels slowly over rough and vegetated surfaces toward rivers and streams.

Impervious surfaces in developed areas, including roofs and parking lots, contribute to stormwater runoff.

water becomes a problem rather than the replenishing resource it should be.

Unfortunately, most traditional control measures do not work very well. Stormwater runoff can also overload local water treatment systems, which in many cases treat sanitary sewage from showers and toilets and stormwater in the same facilities. Water coming in during a rainstorm can exceed the system's capacity, resulting in discharges of mixed sewage and stormwater directly into local lakes, rivers, and streams. In the United States, these combined sewer overflows (CSOs) discharge about 850 billion gallons (3.2 trillion L) of untreated sewage and stormwater in thirty-two states and the District of Columbia every year (EPA 2004a).

CSO discharges can contaminate drinking water supplies, beaches and waterfront parks, and seafood stocks, threatening public health as well as environmental quality. While they are most often found in the Northeast and Midwest, CSOs occur throughout the United States. New York Harbor alone receives more than 27 billion gallons (1 trillion L) of sewage and polluted runoff from an average of 460 CSOs every year (Storm Water Infrastructure Matters [SWIM] Coalition 2008). In King County, Washington, including the city of Seattle, 815 million gallons (3.1 billion L) from eighty-seven CSOs were discharged into local water bodies from June 2007 to May 2008 (King County Department of Natural Resources and Parks 2008). Separate sanitary and stormwater sewer systems do not, unfortunately, magically solve water pollution problems. Sanitary systems can also become overloaded during heavy storms and discharge sewage; the EPA (no date) estimates that this happens about 40,000 times every year.

Green roofs can be part of a more effective approach. Management of stormwater runoff is the green roof benefit that has been most amply documented and validated by research, and stormwater management has been a leading driver of green roof construction in North America as well as in Europe. Green roofs can help to minimize runoff from rooftops in all but the worst storms, and even then, while there will be runoff, there will almost always be less of it from a green roof than from a conventional roof. Rain that is not held by the assembly runs off a green roof more slowly than off a conventional roof, and it moves over a longer time frame, attenuating the intense peak flows of runoff during storms. Water used by plants and evaporated back into the atmosphere never runs off at all.

In temperate areas of North America, such as the northeastern, midwestern, and northwestern United States, even thin green roofs, with about 4 inches (10 cm) of growing medium, usually capture at least half of the annual rainfall and most of the rain that falls in the summer months, when some areas experience frequent storms. In areas with more extreme rainfall pat-

Left: Sewage discharges contaminate water in many urban areas. Photograph by Tom Liptan

Right: Traditional stormwater infrastructure projects using pipes and conveyance are expensive, disruptive, and often ineffective at protecting water quality.

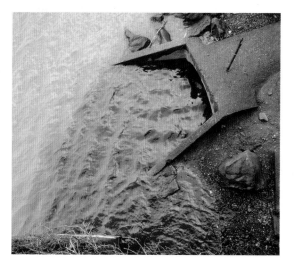

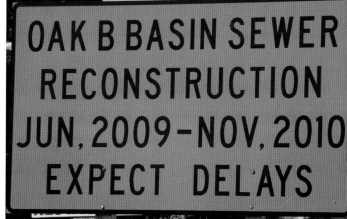

OAK B BASIN SEWER
RECONSTRUCTION
JUN, 2009 – NOV, 2010
EXPECT DELAYS

Green roofs can retain most of the rainfall from all but the largest storms and attenuate peak flows of runoff, easing the burden on sewage systems. This graph shows the runoff from the eastern and western sections of a green roof in Portland, Oregon (gpm, gallons per minute). The green roof reduced the flow of runoff when rainfall was most intense, and it held some of the rainwater and released it at a slower, steadier rate. Graph by Tim Kurtz, City of Portland

terns, such as the arid regions of the southwestern United States or the frequent large rain events of the tropics, the average percentage of runoff potentially captured by a green roof might be higher or lower (EPA 2009a).

In areas where air- or rain-borne pollutants cause problems, stormwater that does drain off a green roof is cleaner in some respects owing to the filtering effect of the plants and medium. Green roofs also help to neutralize runoff from acid rain. Decreasing the volume of runoff and delaying its release also takes some of the pressure off both treatment systems and the bodies of water into which the systems discharge. Runoff from green roofs can carry elevated concentrations of some pollutants, such as phosphorous, potassium, calcium, and magnesium, but these effects might diminish as the roof assembly ages (EPA 2009a). For more detailed information on green roofs and storm-

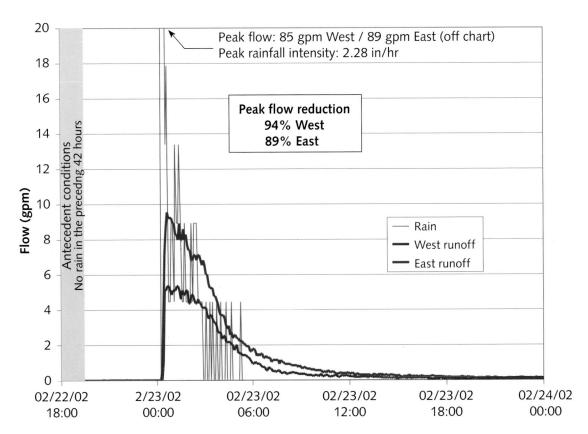

water management, see "Designing for stormwater performance" in chapter 4.

Longer life for the roof membrane

If you have ever been on a roof deck on a hot summer day, you know that the effects of the sun are stronger on top of a building than they are on the ground. The plants, growing medium, and other components of the assembly moderate the temperature on a green roof, not only making it a more pleasant place to be but also protecting the roof's crucial waterproofing membrane from the degrading effects of extreme temperatures and the sun's ultraviolet rays.

The membrane on a conventional flat roof, if not protected by insulation in an inverted application or ballast, often has to be replaced frequently, perhaps after fifteen or twenty years (Luckett 2009a). In Germany, however, the membranes under green roofs built decades ago are intact, and designers there typically plan, conservatively, for a life span of at least thirty to forty years. Other protective approaches, such as insulation installed above the waterproofing membrane and landscapes built over underground structures, also prolong its life. In Portland, Oregon, an intensive planting at grade on top of a parking garage on a fed-

This graph illustrates the surface temperature fluctuations on a green roof, a reflective white roof, and an unprotected black roof between 5 and 14 June 2008. Even on very hot days, the temperature on a green roof remains cooler than on a white roof and much cooler than on a black roof.
Graph by Stuart Gaffin

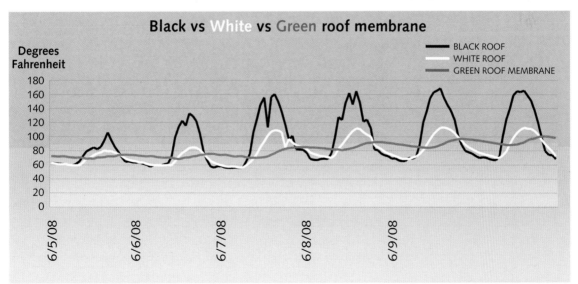

Unprotected membranes are subject to harsh weather conditions, extreme temperature fluctuations, and ultraviolet light. Plants help to maintain the integrity of the green roof assembly that protects the membrane. Ballast is not as stable and can erode, exposing the membrane.

eral building has been functioning flawlessly without a leak in its membrane since 1975 (U.S. General Services Administration [GSA] 2008b). While it is too early to make a conclusive judgment about the life span of green roof components in North American applications, these experiences are encouraging.

Less frequent roof replacement is better for the environment as well as the property owner. Currently about 6 to 9 million tons (5.4 to 8.2 million tonnes) of discarded roofing materials are added to landfills every year in the United States (Cavanaugh 2008).

Lower energy costs

This protection from extreme temperatures can also reduce energy costs for building owners. The mechanisms by which this happens are complex because a green roof is a dynamic system, with varying air and moisture content, biomass, and so on. In some conditions, a green roof can act as an insulator, while in others a thermal mass effect will act to diminish the temperature gradient above and beneath the roof as the system absorbs, then slowly releases, heat.

Research is in its early stages, but some studies suggest that the most significant energy impact of green roofs is the reduction of heat flow into buildings in hot weather, reducing the need for air conditioning and thereby annual energy costs. On some older buildings that lose a lot of heat through the roof, early research suggests that green roofs can also reduce winter heating costs during the coldest months (Bass 2007). Anecdotal evidence from the field is also encouraging. When Illinois-based Aquascape, a manufacturer of components for garden ponds and other water features, installed a 130,000 square foot (12,090 square meter) green roof on its new headquarters building, utility costs went down while the company nearly tripled its space.

Actual savings will vary considerably depending on factors including weather conditions, building characteristics such as roof-to-wall ratio (the higher the ratio, the more significant the impact of the green roof is likely to be, while in a taller building,

The owners of Aquascape, in St. Charles, Illinois, are spending less money on energy for their new green-roofed headquarters.

Exposed waterproofing membranes, even reflective white ones, can degrade more quickly than membranes protected by a green roof assembly.
Photograph by Tom Liptan

the impact of the roof is most significant on the top floor), how the building is operated and used, and the specifics of the green roof assembly. Energy savings alone probably won't justify a green roof on most projects, but they are part of the menu of benefits that makes green roofs attractive as sustainable design tools.

While other cool roof technologies, especially reflective white roofs, are also associated with reduced energy costs, white roofs must be cleaned regularly to stay highly reflective and deliver the best performance. In addition, white roofs do not offer the full spectrum of benefits that properly designed and maintained green roofs do (Rosenzweig et al. 2006). Reflective roofs, often comprising a single-ply membrane, might also be less durable than a green roof or even a conventional roof; more frequent replacement would make such an approach both more expensive and less sustainable (Cavanaugh 2008). "The argument," says green roof engineer and designer Charlie Miller, "is that the white roof is going to go to gray, while the green roof will only get better."

Mitigation of the urban heat island effect

Cities are hotter during the summer than suburban and rural areas because their clustered buildings and paved surfaces hold and slowly release solar radiation, which is known as the urban heat island effect. Managing this phenomenon is a matter not

just of comfort but of public health: Studies have shown that extreme heat is one of the leading causes of natural hazard mortality in the United States, especially among elderly and ill people (Borden and Cutter 2008). Hundreds of people died during a July 1995 heat wave in Chicago (Klinenberg 2002), and more than 14,000 people died in France during the August 2003 heat wave that struck Europe (Larsen 2003). Coping with urban heat by using air conditioning has contributed to increases in residential energy use that have more than offset improvements in efficiency (U.S. Department of Energy, Energy Information Administration 2009), and air conditioning consumes more electricity than any other household appliance or residential end use (U.S. Department of Energy, Energy Information Administration 2001).

Green spaces, including parks, planting beds, and street trees, are cooler owing to evapotranspiration (evaporation plus the release of moisture from plants' leaves), along with the leaves'

Planted areas help keep cities cooler, and green roofs are no exception. Measurements showed that the temperature on this green roof is much lower than that on an adjacent black conventional roof on a hot summer day. Photograph by Joby Carlson, provided courtesy of Jay Golden, National Center of Excellence on SMART Innovations, Arizona State University shading effects. The built urban landscape of most cities includes a huge amount of flat roof area—more than 21,000 acres (8400 ha) in New York City, for example (Rosenzweig et al. 2006)—that could, in many cases, be easily retrofitted to accommodate extensive green roof systems. Research suggests that in green-starved urban areas, green roofs, if widely implemented, could have a significant impact on the urban heat island effect, improving public health (Rosenzweig et al. 2006).

Habitat for urban wildlife

Anecdotal evidence that insects and birds are attracted to green roofs is strong, but the extent to which green roofs can have a significant impact on habitat fragmentation is unclear because few data are available. Research on this subject is still in its early stages, but studies from Europe on mature green roofs suggest that green roofs, when properly designed to accommodate birds' and insects' need for food and shelter, can play an important role in preserving urban biodiversity (Brenneisen 2006).

In the United Kingdom, extensive green roofs are a key part of the London Biodiversity Partnership's action plan to restore the black redstart population (Gedge and Kadas 2005). This protected bird species prefers urban habitats that often lack enough appropriate insect life to support the avian population. Early results have convinced the U.K. Green Building Council and many sustainability advocates that green roofs are among the most effective ways to restore biodiversity to cities (Carus 2009).

In the United States, some green roofs are being designed specifically to attract threatened butterflies and other species, but early research has found a surprisingly high level of diversity even on simple extensive green roofs (Coffman and Waite 2009). For more on designing for habitat, see "Green roofs as wildlife habitat" in chapter 4. It will be interesting to follow the research and see how well this approach works in practice and the extent to which institutional and other owners of habitat-driven projects are willing to engage in the maintenance and sustained observation necessary for the success of this approach.

Green roofs provide some habitat for birds and other wildlife. These stopovers are especially valuable in cities.

Amenity value, aesthetics, and marketing

The cooler temperatures of green roofs in hot weather makes them valuable as amenity spaces for people who live or work in the building below. While simple extensive green roofs are not always designed to be easily accessible to visitors, a sedum roof on a new building, or even a retrofit, can be designed with stepping stones and a patio area (if the building's loading capacity is sufficient), making for a multifunctional and relatively low-cost roof garden. And in a city center, even simple green roofs will usually provide more visual interest for people living or working in neighboring high-rise buildings than conventional roofs, adding welcome color and texture to the urban aesthetic.

Even a simple green roof planted with tough, easy-to-care-for succulents can serve as a beautiful amenity space on an office or apartment building.

Some studies also suggest that green buildings command a premium in the marketplace. A 2008 report by a commercial real estate research company found that buildings certified by the U.S. Green Building Council's Leadership in Energy and Environmental Design (LEED) program or the Department of Energy's Energy Star program fetched higher rents and enjoyed greater occupancy than comparable conventional buildings. The certified buildings, especially LEED buildings, also attracted higher sales prices per square foot. Owners of these buildings also cited the marketing value of the certifications as well as the savings on operational costs (Miller et al. 2008).

There's also some evidence that people prefer to work in green buildings. The U.S. General Services Administration, which owns and leases more than 8000 properties, found in a 2008 postoccupancy evaluation that people who worked in sustainably designed buildings were, on average, 27 percent more satisfied with their surroundings than their counterparts working in a sample drawn from all U.S. commercial buildings. The greenest buildings in the study, however, those certified LEED Gold, performed even better. Their occupants were 34 percent more satisfied (GSA 2008b).

A brief history of green roofs

While roof gardens have long been familiar to North Americans, extensive green roofs migrated here from Europe. In Germany, extensive green roofs have a longer history. Research done there in the 1960s helped to generate a viable market for green roofs starting in the early 1970s. In the 1980s, extensive green roof technology was fine-tuned to meet the need for lighter, less-expensive systems that could be implemented on a wide scale to meet the increasingly urgent need for better stormwater management in densely populated cities. Today the level of green roof coverage in Germany increases by about 145 million square feet (13.5 million square meters) per year (Oberdorfer et al. 2007).

The long life span of green roofs—many of the oldest German roofs are still intact today—and growing evidence of their environmental benefits have made them a popular choice in Europe. These benefits have been compelling enough to European governments that some have put in place an array of subsidies, incentives, and requirements that have greatly expanded the use of green roofs.

In the United States, such policies have always been difficult to implement on the federal level. The green roof industry, comprising a range of professionals from roofers to designers, is not organized as a forceful and monolithic lobby, so there has been no real push for targeted incentives, like those available for renewable energy such as wind and solar power, at the national level. But local incentives are increasingly popular throughout North America. In addition, stronger stormwater management regulations, promulgated under the Clean Water Act and local

Green roofs are common in Germany, Switzerland, and other European countries.

Many buildings owned or managed by the U.S. federal government, including the Department of Transportation in Washington, D.C., have green roofs.

codes, might ultimately make green roofs as common as detention basins are now.

Incentives aside, the U.S. federal government is providing leadership on green roofs, albeit rather quietly. Many agencies now encourage or even require that new construction conform to LEED standards, which awards points for green roofs (U.S. Green Building Council [USGBC] 2009). The EPA has supported the use of low-impact development tools including green roofs and has put green roofs on some of its buildings, including its Region 8 headquarters in Denver and a demonstration project at the agency's Washington, D.C., headquarters.

More government green roofs are likely to come in the wake of the 2007 Energy Independence and Security Act (P. L. 110-140). Section 438 of that law raises the bar for stormwater management on federal government sites with a footprint of 5000 square feet (465 square meters) or more, calling for the maintenance or restoration of predevelopment hydrology to the maximum extent technically feasible through site planning, design, construction, and maintenance strategies. The EPA has interpreted this provision as requiring one of two approaches to site design: either practices that infiltrate, evapotranspirate, harvest, and/or reuse rainfall should be used to prevent runoff from all but the most severe storms, or the project should be designed and built to maintain the predevelopment rate, volume, duration, and temperature for stormwater runoff (EPA 2009b). Section 438 has the potential to validate green building technologies, including green roofs, on a national scale, accelerating their adoption by state and local governments and the private sector (Weinstein and Kloss 2009).

Some state and local governments throughout North America have also established incentives to promote the use of green roofs and other sustainable design technologies in their jurisdictions. In 2009 Toronto approved legislation requiring green roofs for certain new construction projects.

In light of these benefits and incentives, why aren't there more green roofs in North America? Although the number of green roofs here has increased substantially in recent years, green roofs still represent a tiny fraction of total roofs. Reasons for this include novelty, cost, and availability of materials and expertise.

Novelty

Plants on a roof, outside the context of a traditional roof garden, is a tough thing for some people to get their minds around. After all, plants need water to live, and the function of a roof is to keep water out of the building. As the image of a roof in the popular imagination becomes more complex, accommodating roofs with solar panels, wind turbines, and other equipment as well as green roofs, multifunctional roofs should begin to seem more normal.

When Jeanette Stewart proposed replacing a deteriorating conventional roof in her Falls Church, Virginia, condominium community with a green roof, one of the most difficult aspects of the project was convincing her neighbors. Some residents feared that a green roof might collapse, endangering them and their children. They organized a petition drive, and the green roof was eventually installed on another building in the complex. Since

Residents of the Yorktowne Square condominium in Virginia were skeptical at first about a proposed green roof retrofit on one of their buildings. Now it's a source of pride and added value. Photograph by Linda McIntyre

that time, Stewart says, at least one buyer chose a unit based on its location in the green-roofed building.

When Charlie Miller built his first green roof in 1998, extensive green roofs (as opposed to elaborate roof gardens) were virtually unknown in North America. Miller, a stormwater engineer who had learned about green roofs from German colleagues, tested out the technology on the roof of the Philadelphia Fencing Academy, where his daughter was a student. The residents were familiar with the technology, one of them having grown up in Europe.

This simple 3000 square foot (280 square meter) project has endured for more than a decade. The sedums in the original planting palette have been joined by some weeds and grasses, and the 2.75 inches (6.9 cm) of growing medium has shifted around a bit, resulting in thicker and thinner areas, but it is attractive and functioning well. The roof was designed to be low

The Philadelphia Fencing Academy is home to one of the earliest extensive green roofs in North America. Photograph courtesy of Roofscapes

maintenance, and it has received little over the years, so it's constantly evolving.

Cost

Green roofs are more expensive to build than simple conventional roofs. Advocates of green roofs cite the potentially longer life span of green roofs as a justification for the extra expense. This kind of calculation, however, also has to account for maintenance over the life of the roof, which usually will be somewhat more costly and labor-intensive on even an extensive green roof than it would for a conventional roof.

But a green roof is more than just a way to keep water out of the building. It can offset other engineering costs associated with a building project, such as stormwater detention systems. For many people, the full spectrum of benefits, public as well as private, will justify the additional costs. Incentives can quantify and

Prices for green roof installations can vary considerably. This large extensive green roof in Chicago, where the industry is fairly competitive, was installed for about $7 per square foot (about 0.1 square meter). But costs for even simple projects like this can be surprisingly high.

monetize these benefits. As the North American green roof industry grows and suppliers multiply and compete, prices are likely to come down (Philippi 2006). But for now, extensive green roofs are often considered premium products and priced accordingly, to the puzzlement and frustration of many in the industry. In some cases extensive green roofs cost more to install than elaborate roof gardens. Building owners should shop around and choose designers and installers who can deliver in an economical fashion. For more detail on navigating the green roof marketplace, see chapter 3.

Availability of materials and expertise

Back in 2000, when Dansko shoe company founder Peter Kjellerup wanted to build a new headquarters in Pennsylvania with a green roof and other sustainable features, he and his colleagues had a difficult time finding people to help and appropriate materials. Fortunately, Kjellerup, drawing upon his own research and

The green roofs on the Dansko headquarters have been a successful element in the company's sustainability strategy.

the resources of the regional green building council, was eventually able to assemble a motivated project team that had "a real desire to learn."

"It's much different now," he says of the green building landscape. "It's much more doable now than when we started this building. The price tag is lower, too. With higher energy costs it's easier to see that it pays off."

In 2002 Gerding Edlen Development in Portland, Oregon, working with other local firms, started design on a green roof on part of a mixed-use project in the city's Pearl District. Nobody on the project team had any green roof experience, appropriate materials were difficult to find, and Portland's technical assistance program, of which the project team made use, was in its early days. So it's not surprising that the team's first attempt was beset by problems.

Remediation was insufficient, so eventually the team, having learned from its mistakes the first time around, started over, redesigning the whole assembly and working with a knowledgeable local horticulturist. Gerding Edlen has continued to use green roofs on its projects, and partner Dennis Wilde says success is easier to achieve for a variety of reasons: appropriate growing medium is easier to find; the firm's general contractor has become more proficient at controlling the delivery of materials and the installation process; local landscape architects have developed a better understanding of what works and what does not in Portland's climate, which is very wet in winter and very dry in summer; the local design community is more knowledgeable and therefore less susceptible to aggressive sales pitches; and the firm has worked with local landscape companies to develop better maintenance practices.

Designers, builders, and property owners considering green

This green roof in the Pearl District of Portland, Oregon, was part of the project team's learning curve. It's now attractive and functioning well.

roofs in other areas might agree with these assessments, but increased interest in green roofs, coupled with the lack of industry standards and postinstallation evaluation of performance, has created some understandable confusion in the marketplace, especially for a building owner or client who is unfamiliar with the technology. There is, at this time, no *Consumer Reports*–type reference to help navigate conflicting claims by designers, installers, and manufacturers. But arming yourself with basic information, at the earliest stages of the design process, is one way to navigate through varying approaches and conflicting claims. Another is careful selection of an experienced project team. For more detailed information on the status and outlook for green roof construction in North America, see chapter 3.

Will green roofs remain a small niche, or are their numbers likely to increase?

The recent surge in the popularity of green building and marketing, in the midst of both a building boom and early signs of an urban infrastructure crisis, put green roofs in the spotlight. This attention has highlighted the difficulties associated with green roof design and installation as well as the advantages. Some projects were built without the proper experience or attention to the particular requirements of green roofs, and in some cases the desire for LEED certification or other ecologically correct credentials drove projects to the detriment of sensible design.

There are now hundreds of green roofs in North America, and these projects—whether they are thriving or failing—offer the best lessons for people interested in green roof design, construction, and maintenance. If you are considering a green roof for your project, as either a client or a designer, you would be well served to see as many green roofs and learn as much about them as possible so you can make an informed decision about your own project. Don't assume that glamorous photos you might have seen on a website, in a magazine, or as part of an awards ceremony are representative of the way the roof looks currently, in all seasons, or without regular maintenance.

Green roofs show promise, but many of their potential benefits can only be realized if they are built on a large scale. In North America, we've got a long way to go.

Even in light of a green roof's multifaceted package of potential benefits, building one is not a decision to be made lightly or as an afterthought. On the design and installation side, a successful green roof is the result of a truly multidisciplinary process, one that starts with the understanding that a green roof is a living system, not just part of a building. For the client, keeping a green roof thriving, while not usually difficult if done regularly and properly, is a long-term commitment. Being mindful of the challenges, as well as the payoffs, at the earliest stages of a project will greatly increase the likelihood of success.

The green roof assembly, all of
the elements above the roof's
waterproofing membrane, is
known as the overburden.

2 Anatomy of a Green Roof Assembly

Key Points

- A successful green roof requires the selection of growing medium and plants that will work with the site, fulfill the project's design intent, and thrive over the long term with the resources available for maintenance.
- Attention to standard roofing issues, including structural loading, waterproofing, and drainage, is also an integral part of green roof design.

A green roof assembly consists of both horticultural elements and elements more commonly associated with traditional roofing than with planted systems. The latter are as important as the former—a leaking green roof with healthy plants is a compromised or failed green roof project.

In roofing terminology, the whole green roof assembly above the waterproofing membrane is known as the overburden. The most basic green parts of a green roof are the growing medium

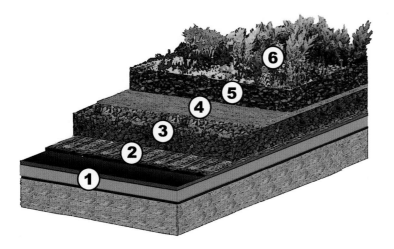

Each layer of a green roof assembly contributes to its function.

1 Roof deck, insulation, waterproofing
2 Protection and storage layer
3 Drainage layer
4 Root-permeable filter layer
5 Extensive growing media
6 Plants, vegetation

Illustration by Green Roof Service LLC

and plants. The elements that ensure the structural integrity of the building are the roof deck and the waterproofing membrane. Almost every green roof will have some kind of drainage layer in addition to the primary and secondary (overflow) drains that are part of any roofing system (National Roofing Contractors Association [NRCA] 2009). Other layers will vary. Synthetic sheets or fabrics might be used to stop the migration of fine particles into the drainage layer, retain extra moisture, or protect the membrane from damage by roots. Biodegradable netting or blankets might be used to prevent erosion immediately after installation. Insulation might be installed above the membrane rather than under the roof deck.

The particulars of the assembly should always be determined by the requirements and objectives of the project, the properties of the components, and their ability to work together as an engineered system for optimal performance. Designs and specifications for green roof assemblies should not be copied and pasted or repeated by rote from project to project.

The living part of the green roof: growing medium

Growing medium is to plants on a green roof what soil is to plants in a garden, and some industry professionals even refer to the medium as "soil." But most of the medium used on extensive green roofs bears little resemblance to garden or field soil. It's not fine-textured, soft, and earthy. When it's wet, medium does not get muddy or sticky. Most of its particles are quite a bit larger than the sand, silt, and clay that comprise soil, and it has a rockier look and feel.

In countries such as Germany, where green roofs are common, inputs such as growing medium are thoroughly tested against well-established standards before they are approved for sale in the marketplace. Climate conditions are also more consistent because the land area of the country is relatively small, requiring fewer variations in the characteristics and performance of the material.

But in the geographically enormous, young, and laissez-faire

Green roof growing medium plays a role similar to that of field or garden soil, but it's composed of mineral aggregates and only a small amount of organic material.

green roof culture of North America, it's more difficult to sort through the conflicting claims of various vendors and manufacturers. The plants often used on green roofs and their cultural requirements might be unfamiliar to designers and horticulturists accustomed to working at grade. Proper specification of the medium can be similarly difficult because its characteristics are so different from those of field soil.

The design intent and conditions on the site will guide the specific qualities and depth of medium required on any given project. Intensive roof gardens, for example, planted primarily with perennials, shrubs, and trees, could require completely dif-

A comparison of the required properties of green roof medium versus those of field soils and nursery plant medium

Green Roof Medium	Field Soils	Nursery Medium
lightweight with minimum compressibility	too heavy	compressible and unstable
structurally stable	migration of fine particles	sequestration of nutrients
excellent long-term performance and permeability	long-term permeability problems	long-term permeability problems

Table courtesy of Roofscapes

ferent soils and other components than extensive green roofs planted with hardy succulents, and they will have to be deeper to accommodate those root systems. But, in general, growing medium should have the following qualities: good and consistent drainage and aeration; a structure that enables it to hold water for uptake by plants; the ability to make nutrients accessible to plant roots through cation exchange capacity; resistance to decomposition and compression; a light weight; and physical and chemical stability (Friedrich 2005). While actual sterility is difficult to achieve, the medium should also be as free as possible of weed seeds, because weeds can quickly take over a newly planted green roof before desired plants are well established.

Materials vary, and so do their carbon footprints

Growing medium for extensive green roofs planted primarily with hardy succulents usually comprises at least 80 percent coarse lightweight mineral aggregate. These materials, some of which are added to cement to make concrete lighter, form the basis of the medium's structure, stability, and longevity without adding a lot of weight. Commonly used aggregates include expanded clay, shale, or slate (the materials are heated to very high temperatures in a kiln to a point at which they expand into a lightweight, pop-

Expanded and volcanic materials can be used together in growing medium blends to take advantage of the benefits of each.

corn-like form while retaining strength and density) and volcanic material such as pumice. Each of these materials consists of particles with a sponge-like appearance; the voids hold air and organic material and increase the particle's surface area, slowing the movement of water.

Preferred aggregate materials for green roof medium vary somewhat by region. Pumice, for example, is widely available in the Pacific Northwest owing to nearby volcanoes in the Cascade Range. It's also commonly used on the East Coast, where it has usually been shipped from Greece or Iceland. It's light (about 40 pounds per cubic foot [640.7 kg per cubic meter] dry, 47 pounds [752.9 kg] saturated; Friedrich 2005), durable, and easy to handle, and the embodied energy required to process it is low. But away from the coasts, transportation costs can make it prohibitively expensive compared to expanded materials and increase its carbon footprint.

Some research has found that expanded clay, with its better water-holding capacity and promotion of cation exchange, supports plants better than expanded shale on an unirrigated extensive green roof, while expanded shale might be preferable in areas with a lot of rain, especially acid rain (EPA 2009a). But designers and specifiers seeking to use the most sustainable materials should be aware that expanded aggregates require a lot of energy to produce and, when not locally available, to transport. They are also heavier than volcanic materials: expanded clay weighs about 40 pounds per cubic foot (640.7 kg per cubic meter) dry, 54 pounds (865.0 kg) saturated while expanded shale weighs about 44 pounds per cubic foot (704.8 kg per cubic meter) dry and 58 pounds (929.1 kg) saturated (Friedrich 2005). This might make these aggregates less desirable for both retrofits, when loading capacity is often restricted, and on some new construction, when enhancing the structure can be expensive and resource-intensive.

While some green roof projects have used medium blends that include extremely lightweight materials such as perlite or Styrofoam in an effort to keep the weight of the system low, these materials lack sufficient compression strength to support the system over time and are so light they will often easily blow off a roof (Beattie and Berghage 2004). Sand, sometimes found in green roof medium blends, is very heavy, typically 90 pounds per cubic foot (1441.6 kg per cubic meter) dry and 130 pounds (2082.4 kg) wet, and retains few plant-available nutrients (Friedrich 2005). Sand should be used sparingly, if at all, on most extensive green roofs.

Use available benchmarks to select the right blend

There are few standards of North American origin to assist in the selection and specification of growing medium. ASTM International (formerly known as the American Society for Testing and Materials) has established a green roof task force and recently issued five testing methods that provide some guidance. These include E2399, Standard Test Method for Maximum Media Density for Dead Load Analysis, which also measures the moisture retention potential and saturated water permeability of medium (Roofscapes, no date).

The most comprehensive guidelines available are published by the German Landscape Research, Development, and Construction Society, known by the initials FLL (for Forschungsgesellschaft Landschaftsentwicklung Landschaftsbau). The guidelines, which are frequently updated and available in English, cover the planning, construction, and maintenance of green roofs. They are a valuable source of technical information and reference values for green roof materials and installation, and the information is presented in a clear, well-organized, and accessible format.

Growing medium is discussed in the guidelines' section on the "vegetation support course." This section includes helpful information on appropriate granulometric distribution (particle sizes), levels of organic matter, and other properties. The suggested ranges are flexible enough to realize a variety of design intents in different regions and provide a good starting point for specifying growing medium.

Medium that complies with FLL guidelines is available from many North American sources. To make sure the medium you specify is fine-tuned to your requirements, or to confirm that a vendor's medium complies with the stated specifications, testing of a medium's physical (density, air-filled porosity, water-holding capacity, hydraulic conductivity, and particle size distribution) and chemical (organic content, pH, soluble salts, nutrient content) properties is also available from various labs. Green roof medium, with its large particles and largely mineral character, is tested by methods different from traditional soil analysis, so testing is not as widely available. The FLL has developed a set of specific tests and methods (such as compacting the medium with a proctor hammer). At the time of this writing, only Penn State University uses the full range of FLL test methods as well as those available from ASTM (Penn State University Agriculture Analytic Services Lab, no date).

Many experienced green roof designers and installers in North America have used commercially available FLL medium with considerable success. The qualities of growing medium should, however, take into account regional considerations and the desired plant palette to the fullest extent possible. This might require some modification of the guidelines in the specifications.

For example, in the eastern United States, acid rain can lower the pH of the medium to the point at which it is difficult for plants to take up nutrients. In this case the chemical stability of the medium takes on added importance. In addition, according to Robert Berghage, the FLL guidelines tend to overestimate the air-filled porosity of the media particles. The FLL guidelines also allow a level of fine particles that might pose problems in areas that typically get a lot of rain (more than about 50 inches [125 cm] per year). In such places, green roofs with an FLL-type medium can hold too much water, adding weight to the system and possibly providing a hospitable environment for weeds.

However, some have experienced the opposite problem. Landscape architect Jeffrey Bruce, who works on projects in climates ranging from northern Minnesota to desert areas, finds that FLL medium is too dry and granular. Bruce usually custom blends growing medium for his projects, an approach that is ideal for optimal performance but might not be realistic for smaller projects or for green roofs installed purely in response to stormwater codes and requirements.

The FLL guidelines themselves clearly state that special or local conditions might require adjustment. In a market lacking a lot of credible reference points, any set that has been tested in both the lab and the field, over decades, is invaluable, even if not every detail is directly transferable. "The big advantage of the FLL guidelines is the combination of setting clear reference values and defining precise testing methods and procedures, which guarantee the comparability of results," says green roof consultant Peter Philippi. "But the green roof system, and the most important of all, the plant selection, has to be adjusted to local conditions. So your green roof might fail, even though all components fit to FLL standards. Nevertheless, following the FLL requirements can eliminate a lot of potential sources of failure."

Be picky about your supplier

Growing medium is usually purchased from suppliers who offer different blends for intensive and extensive projects, often formulated according to FLL guidelines. Some offer custom blends for specific performance requirements.

Designers and installers who need a supply of consistent, high-quality green roof medium should cultivate a relationship with their supplier, including at least one visit to the site. Careless or poor storage or handling on the site can contaminate otherwise good growing medium. Responsible suppliers will keep a clean site to avoid weed and other seeds from blowing into the

A responsible blender will keep a clean site to avoid contaminating the growing medium with weed seeds.

medium, and they will protect it from contamination during delivery and installation. It's reasonable to ask your supplier for a weed germination test.

They will also make sure that compost included in the blend has been processed long enough to be free of weed seeds and chemical contaminants. Compost that is not completely broken down consumes nitrogen and oxygen, which can rob nutrients from plants, damaging or killing them (Friedrich 2005). Testing protocols are available from the United States Composting Council and should be used (Luckett 2009a).

Most good blenders will provide cutsheets detailing performance information, but due diligence is still required. "Visit other installations, see how they are doing, talk to clients," says Jeffrey Bruce. "Talk to references, find out what the soil specification is, its bulk density and infiltration rate. When you're on the site, pull a sample and send it to a lab." Bruce says he and his colleagues do this regularly and often find that the product does not meet the represented specification. Reliable performance data are especially important, he says, for thinner-profile extensive roofs. "As you reach extremes, you have opportunities for greater failures."

Deeper is not necessarily better

The appropriate depth of the medium will depend on many factors, including the plant palette, typical rainfall and aridity in the region, and desired stormwater performance. In Germany, 3 inches (7.5 cm) of granular material (this can comprise both growth and drainage aggregates) works well, providing enough support for desired plants but not so much as to increase weed pressure. Three to 4 inches (7.5 to 10 cm) can also work well for extensive green roofs in the mid-Atlantic, New England, and Great Lakes regions, while in hotter, drier regions a minimum of 6 inches (15 cm) will often be needed to support plants (Miller 2008). In very hot and dry regions such as the American Southwest, 8 to 12 inches (20 to 30 cm) or more, plus a topdressing of mulch, might be necessary (Lenart 2009).

The benefits of deeper medium are not unlimited, however, even for stormwater performance. Three to 4 inches (7.5 to 10 cm) will usually manage about 80 percent of rainfall from heavy summer storms; going deeper can provide some added benefits, but beyond this point the benefits are often disproportionate to the added costs. A deeper system can even be counterproductive: an 18-month study of five green roof test plots in Seattle found that 8 inches (20 cm) of medium did not allow captured rainfall to evaporate quickly enough for the system to fully drain between storms, diminishing its effectiveness as a stormwater management tool (Gangnes 2007). For more detail on the impact of depth on plant health and stormwater management, see chapter 4.

Go easy on the organic matter

It seems counterintuitive for a horticultural environment, but most green roof medium for extensive projects should not have a very high organic content. Organic matter, while it adds some water-holding and cation exchange capacity, decomposes quickly, decreasing volume and potentially compromising drainage (Friedrich 2005). In most cases organic material should comprise only up to 20 percent of the medium by volume for extensive green roofs planted in late summer or autumn, and 10 percent is sufficient for spring planting. When plants are established and mature, a stable and healthy extensive green roof system usually

A reliable source of compost, free from contaminants, is essential for growing medium. Spent substrate from mushroom cultivation is harvested from this field and blended with other components.

comprises about 2 to 5 percent organic matter by weight (Beattie and Berghage 2004).

A good blender of green roof medium will have a reliable and consistent source of compost. Materials used include leaf mold, composted animal waste and sewage sludge, worm castings, and spent substrate from mushroom cultivation. Compost that includes sewage sludge should be used with caution, if at all, because its particle distribution might be too fine to maintain porosity and it can also contain heavy metals and pathogens (Friedrich 2005). Different substances will have different nutrient levels and varying rates of decay. Those that decay too quickly can compromise the stability of the system, possibly resulting in an almost total loss of porosity. The medium's porosity should be maintained for five years while the plants mature. The U.S. Composting Council offers a testing assurance program, and the organization's Test Methods for Composting and Compost can provide addition guidance (U.S. Composting Council, no date).

The organic material blended into the medium should be free of contaminants such as residual herbicides. Their impact is exaggerated in the less biodynamic environment of medium as opposed to field or garden soil. Ask for certification from your supplier. Some designers and installers use medium inoculated with mycorrhizal fungi to promote good establishment, but re-

A bad medium blend is bad news for green roof plants.

search suggests that microbiological communities will establish on their own; at most this provides only a jump-start.

Early in the life of a green roof, runoff usually has higher concentrations of some nutrients. This is typical of water leached from any newly planted landscape and is likely the result of organic matter in the medium. These higher concentrations can be visible in the form of rusty-looking humic acid stains on paved areas near downspouts. The impact on water quality, however, probably is minimal, because total runoff is so much less and concentrations might diminish as the system stabilizes over time (EPA 2009a). Once the roots have spread through the medium, they will absorb that humic acid.

Ordering and specifying

To calculate the amount of medium to order, multiply the depth of medium in inches by the square footage of the roof and divide by 324 to get the number of cubic yards. Some designers recommend ordering an extra 10 to 20 percent to account for settling and compaction (Rooflite Green Roof Media, no date). This example provides a good benchmark for specification (sample specification courtesy of Roofscapes):

A. Extensive growth media is a mixture of mineral and organic components that satisfies the following specifications:

Noncapillary pore space at maximum water capacity (ASTM-E2399) ≥ 10 percent

Maximum water capacity (ASTM-E2399) ≥ 10 percent

Density at maximum water capacity (ASTM-E2399) ≤ 75 pounds per cubic foot (1200 kg per cubic meter)

Saturated hydraulic conductivity (ASTM-E2399) 0.10–1.0 inches (0.25–2.5 cm) per minute

Alkalinity, $CaCO_3$ equivalents (MSA) 2.5 percent

Total organic matter, loss on ignition method (MSA) 4–10 percent (dry weight)

pH (RCSTP) 6.5–8.0 soluble

Salts (DPTA saturated paste extraction; RCSTP) ≤ 6 mmhos/cm

Organic supplements (compost, peat moss, etc.) with a

combined respiration rate (TMECC 05.08, B) ≤ 1 mg
CO_2 per gram total organic matter per day

Cation exchange capacity (MSA) ≥ 10 meq per 100 g

Grain-size distribution of the mineral fraction
(ASTM-D422)

    Clay fraction (2 micron) ≤ 2 percent
    Passing US#200 sieve (i.e., silt fraction) ≤ 5 percent
    Passing US#60 sieve ≤ 10 percent
    Passing US#18 sieve 5–50 percent
    Passing ⅛-inch sieve 30–80 percent
    Passing ⅜-inch sieve 75–100 percent

Total nitrogen, TKN (MSA) 25–100 ppm

Phosphorus, P_2O_5 (Mehlich III) 20–200 ppm

Potassium, K_2O (Mehlich III) ≥ 150 ppm

Other macro- and micronutrients should be incorporated
in the formulation in initial proportions suitable for
supporting the specified planting.

B. The medium should be thoroughly blended at a batch facility. Moisten, as required, to prevent separation and excessive
dusting during installation. Quality control samples should
be collected for each 100 cubic yards (76.5 cubic meters) provided to the job. These samples should be sealed in 2-gallon
(7.6-L) water-tight containers and held by the contractor for
inspection by the owner's representative.

The living part of the green roof: plants

Plants are the point of a green roof, and not just because they
look nice. Research indicates that a roof with actively growing
plants provides superior stormwater retention compared to an
equivalent ballast roof (EPA 2009a). Plants that establish quickly
and live for a long time are a crucial component in a project's success. It's important to remember, however, that a roof environment bears little resemblance to a garden at grade. Stressors such
as heat, sunlight, and wind are much more intense on a roof, and
soil qualities that are valuable at grade (such as a high organic
content) can be unwelcome on a roof (too much organic matter in
growing medium can promote weed pressure and lead to degra-

dation and loss of volume). Many plants cannot live, let alone thrive, in such an environment.

A green roof plant has to bind the medium together with a root system that persists all year round to prevent wind scour and provide horizontal continuity to the system, improving its function and efficiency. It has to pump water from the medium to the atmosphere through evapotranspiration, but at the same time it must be able to survive periods when the medium is dry. Its foli-

Tough green roof plants such as these sedums can often grow even when conditions are not ideal. This growing medium has an undesirably high level of fine particles; most plant species would have died under such conditions.

Other sturdy plants such as *Opuntia* can also be good candidates for a green roof environment.

age must have enough surface area to shade the medium, preventing the germination of weed seeds. It should be long lived, obviating the need for wasteful and expensive replacement. Most important, it should perform the desired service for the client and perhaps the broader community as well, providing water storage and movement, cooling, food for pollinators, habitat, and/or beauty.

Characteristics of successful green roof plants include ease of establishment, a shallow lateral root system, low nutrient and maintenance requirements, resistance to damage from insects and disease, lack of windborne seeds, and light weight at maturity. These qualities are most easily found in hardy succulents including *Sedum*, *Sempervivum*, *Talinum*, *Jovibarba*, and *Delosperma*, which effectively conserve and store water in their leaves. Some cacti, such as *Opuntia*, also make good green roof plants.

Don't vilify sedums

Of these genera, *Sedum* species are the most widely adaptable and useful on green roofs. In fact "sedum" has become a kind of shorthand for any extensive green roof plant. Some designers, failing to understand the plant's physiology and the diversity within the genus, specify sedums irrespective of the climate or design intent. Others use "sedum roof" or even "sedum monoculture" in a pejorative sense, bemoaning a perceived lack of biodiversity and ecological benefits. This characterization is horticulturally incorrect: The term monoculture only applies to the use of one species over a wide geographic range and cannot be applied accurately at the genera level.

The genus *Sedum* comprises more than 400 species and thousands of varieties with a geographic distribution throughout the Northern Hemisphere. There are annual species such as *Sedum pulchellum* and long-lived perennial species such as *Sedum spurium*. *Sedum spathulifolium* is a host plant for butterfly species such as the red admiral (*Vanessa atalanta*), painted lady (*Vanessa cardui*), and small Apollo (*Parnassius phoebus*). Designers and others specifying green roof plants must have a clear understanding of plant performance relative to the project objectives and the conditions on site.

The simple reason for the widespread use of *Sedum* species is their ability to tolerate a wide range of conditions relative to other genera. Most have the ability to change their metabolism to adapt to droughts and then change back when moisture is plentiful. This survival skill allows sedums to stay alive when most other plants perish. During the summer, plants on an extensive green roof generally use all available water within three to six days after irrigation or a rainfall. Any moisture that remains in

Sedum album

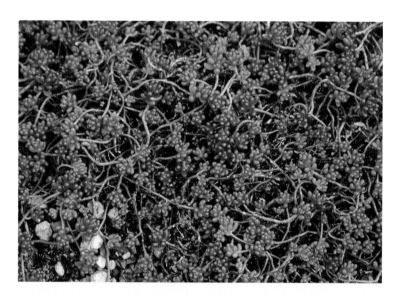

Sedum album subsp. *teretifolium* 'Murale'

the system is very tightly held in the medium. At this point, if moisture levels are not replenished, plants go into drought response, a kind of survival mode. Hardy succulents such as *Sedum* species cease daytime evapotranspiration, effectively conserving water in their tissue, while most herbaceous plants, attempting to minimize surface exposure, wilt and shortly thereafter die. Even plants that go dormant rather than dying completely, such as some grass species, take longer to regrow, and they produce a lot

Sedum kamtschaticum

Sedum kamtschaticum var. *floriferum* 'Weihenstephaner Gold'

of desiccated biomass, which in addition to being unattractive can be a fire hazard in some areas. Appropriate herbaceous plants can certainly be used on an extensive green roof, but both the specifier and the owner must understand that the effort and resources necessary to maintain those plants will almost always be higher than if succulents were used.

Sedum album, *S. album* subsp. *teretifolium* 'Murale,' *S. kamtschaticum*, *S. kamtschaticum* var. *floriferum* 'Weihenstephaner Gold',

Sedum sexangulare

Sedum spurium 'Fuldaglut'

S. sexangulare, and *S. spurium* 'Fuldaglut' are good workhorse species that have proven tough, persistent, and highly adaptable in green roof applications.

Amp up your aesthetics with non-succulents

Annuals, perennials, grasses, and bulbs can all be used on an extensive green roof. Annuals, usually planted as seeds, add quick color to a green roof and can help fill in bare spots, keeping weed pressure down. Perennials and grasses can be planted in protected or mounded areas on roofs that are primarily planted with hardy succulents to add color and texture. Bulbs bring a welcome pop of color in early spring.

Plant selection for a green roof project should be based on the design intent for both aesthetics and function, budget and maintenance considerations, the accessibility and likely level of use by people who live or work in the building, and macro- and microclimates on site. For more detail on green roof plant palettes, see "Green roofs as amenity spaces" in chapter 4.

While the hardiness and heat zone maps used by gardeners can provide some broad initial guidance when selecting green

These small bulbs have been used with success on some extensive green roofs:

Allium neapolitanum
Allium oreophilum
Crocus chrysanthus
Crocus tommasinianus
Iris humilis
Iris reticulata
Muscari comosum
Narcissus willkommii
Scilla bifolia
Scilla siberica
Tulipa humilis

Small bulbs such as species tulips can be used on extensive green roofs for a pop of spring color.

roof plants, conditions are so different on top of a building and microclimates are so important that the utility of these guidelines is limited. A building's aspect relative to the sun, its exposure to wind, and the effectiveness of its insulation, among other things, mean that a roof might exist in a different U.S. Department of Agriculture hardiness zone than its geographical region. The heat zone map developed by the American Horticultural Society is of limited use in green roof design, but it can help in some instances—for example, most plants will experience stress at temperatures above 85°F (30°C), so it can be helpful to know how many days a year, on average, a place typically has weather that hot. The European Köppen-Geiger climate classification map can also help to determine weather patterns and rainfall versus potential evaporation.

Specifying common green roof plants: plugs, cuttings, and seeds

As with gardens at grade, green roof plants best adapt to their new environment and are most successful over the long term when they are planted at a juvenile stage. Although it might seem intuitive that larger plants in large containers would jump-start a green roof project, reducing weed pressure and making it look lush right away, these containers do not work well on an extensive green roof. The introduction of large amounts of nursery medium in containers will change the soil composition of the roof, ruining a carefully considered specification.

Plants raised to maturity in nursery soil, with its high organic content and fine particles, will not adapt well to the austere environment provided by green roof growing medium, and large plants are rarely able to adapt to the harsh conditions on a roof. Nursery soil can dry out very quickly and become hydrophobic, trapping roots. The exposed soil mix from nursery pots can also carry in weeds and, being ill-suited to the rooftop environment, can devolve into a zone of death in which nothing desirable will grow. Even if large plants were suitable for use on a green roof, the added weight and expense of such an approach would make it untenable for most projects.

Specifiers should have a good understanding of which species are available in the nursery trade and which are not. For a functional extensive project, plants should be specified at the species level—specifying cultivars might cause supply and substitution problems that can delay installation. Using species not commonly available will require custom propagation, which will usually increase the cost of plants and require more money up front. Custom propagation can also stretch out the timeline of a project.

Local conditions, such as hurricane season around the Gulf of Mexico, severe summers in the American Southwest, and severe winters in the north, can affect planting. To make sure plants are installed at an appropriate time that will allow them to properly establish, planting time might have to be specified and might ideally take place after most other project work is finished.

The methods of planting common green roof plants—as cuttings, plugs, or seeds—are not mutually exclusive. Plugs can be oversown with cuttings and seeds can be oversown on plugs and cuttings as a cost-effective way to get faster plant cover and add visual interest.

Cuttings are bits of plant that root easily and become separate plants. This is a less complex process for common green roof plants than, say, rooting a woody plant for which you need two

Plants raised in nursery pots often have a difficult time adapting to a green roof environment. The exposed soil can carry in weeds and dry out completely, becoming a zone of horticultural death.

Cuttings of *Sedum* species root quickly and easily.

buds. Many *Sedum* species root so easily as cuttings that occasional foot traffic that breaks off small pieces of stem is a good way to add more plants. They must be shipped under refrigeration during hot periods and quickly planted on arrival at the site, so good communication between the supplier and installer is crucial. But cuttings are relatively inexpensive and, when properly installed, establish very quickly. It is difficult or impossible, however, to realize a controlled or detailed planting design with cuttings, and plant choices are limited to *Sedum* and *Delosperma* species. They require some expertise to install, and cannot be used when plants are dormant.

Cuttings are usually installed at a rate of 25 to 50 pounds (11.4 to 22.8 kg) per 1000 square feet (92 square meters). More cuttings will, of course, mean quicker cover. They can be used alone or in combination with plugs and seeds. Cuttings will usually arrive in boxes, which should be opened and immediately inspected for any damage so the supplier can be contacted and problems resolved within the installation timeframe.

Cuttings should be broadcast on medium that has been thoroughly wetted to assure they have good surface contact with the moisture they will need to start the establishment process. Photodegradable netting, jute, or a tackifier can help keep cuttings in place until roots develop.

Cuttings are usually shipped in boxes under refrigerated conditions.

Cuttings are broadcast over the growing medium and root quickly if the medium is kept moist.
Photograph courtesy of Furbish Company

Because different species will establish at different rates and adapt to microclimates with different degrees of success, a mix of species should be applied. Using more species will provide greater variety in texture and appearance as well as insurance against species that do not respond well to the conditions on site. Cuttings can also be used after installation, during maintenance, to fill in bare spots.

Plugs are small plants with established root systems, essentially tiny container plants. They are packed and transported in 10- by 20-inch (25- by 50-cm) nursery trays most often comprising 36, 50, or 72 plants. The number of plants in the tray also denotes the size of the plugs—the higher the number, the smaller the plant. Plugs are also available in different depths. Try to find plugs as close to the depth of your growing medium as possible to maximize the interface between the roots and the assembly.

A cutting mix using only a few species will give a roof a relatively uniform appearance.

Below: Using a greater variety of species provides diversity of color and texture. Using more species also increases the likelihood that the mix includes plants that will respond well to site conditions and establish quickly and easily.

Plugs of hardy succulent plants such as sedums do well when planted in a 72 size. Although they are available as smaller plants (such as 108 to a tray), these require more effort and expertise to plant. Grasses are usually sold in larger sizes such as 36 or 50.

Plugs allow for more ambitious planting designs, though the growth rate of the different plants should be considered when specifying quantity to provide greater consistency in plant cover

Plug trays are stacked on pallets for shipping. They should be unpacked and spread out in a single layer as soon as possible after receipt.

Below: Plugs come in different sizes and depths.

during the establishment phase. Plugs are usually planted at a density of one or two per square foot (10 to 20 per square meter). They can be planted more densely for quicker establishment, but there is little benefit in using more than four plugs per square foot (40 per square meter). Like all green roof plants, they should not be mulched.

Results will vary depending on climate, time of planting, and other variables, but here's a good rule of thumb for speci-

Talinum calycinum seedlings

Phacelia campanularia seedlings

fying plugs to achieve about 85 percent coverage: two plugs per square foot will take about 12 to 18 months, three plugs per square foot will take about 9 to 12 months, and four plugs per square foot will take about 6 to 9 months.

Planting a green roof exclusively with seeds is not recommended because plants would take too long to establish, leaving the roof vulnerable to weed pressure and other disturbances. But oversowing a roof with perennial or annual seeds is a good way to experiment with colorful accent plants and to fill in open areas while plugs or cuttings establish or when bare spots appear. Rapidly germinating drought-tolerant species such as *Arctotis acaulis*, *Arctotis hirsuta*, *Dorotheanthus bellidiformis*, *Eschscholzia californica*, *Phacelia campanularia*, *Portulaca pilosa*, and *Talinum calycinum* are good choices for oversowing. Seeds sown in very early spring or autumn will germinate at higher rates. As with cuttings, good surface moisture is important to getting seeds off to a good start. Like other green roof components, seeds should be sourced from a reliable supplier who will certify their viability.

Prevegetated installation options

On a green roof that is built in place, plugs or cuttings are planted after the rest of the system is installed and the growing medium is in place and spread out. Sometimes, however, the logistics of a project or other concerns dictate that plant establishment take place off-site. In such cases, pregrown mats and modules are available.

Mats are similar to sod. The plants, almost always exclusively sedums, which can withstand the stress involved in the process, are grown in the field, then cut into strips, rolled, and quickly transported to the green roof site, where they are unfurled and laid on top of a layer of growing medium. Mats limit the plant palette and potential design effects. They are heavy and somewhat difficult to transport and install, making them more expensive than cuttings or plugs. They usually need irrigation during establishment so they do not dry out and shrink, potentially exposing the roof's waterproofing membrane. But mats offer a good solution for windy situations and those with steeper slopes, and for projects on which the client wants rapid uniform plant cover.

Above: Mats are like sod consisting of succulent plants rather than turfgrass.

Right: Newly installed mats should be irrigated in dry weather. They can dry out severely, killing plants and sometimes shrinking enough to expose and potentially damage other roof components.

Pregrown mats were used as a lightweight, wind-resistant application on a green roof retrofit project on the PECO headquarters in Philadelphia. Photograph courtesy of Roofscapes

Some also consider mats the most effective way to prevent weeds on a new green roof (Miller 2009a).

At 45,000 square feet (4185 square meters), the green roof on the headquarters building of PECO, the Philadelphia electric and gas utility company, is the largest green roof in Pennsylvania. It was installed as a retrofit in late 2008. The site is very windy, a situation occasionally exacerbated by the comings and goings of helicopters, as there is a helipad on the roof.

Originally, this roof was going to be planted with cuttings. But the design team decided that in view of the late season installation and high wind pressure, mats were a better approach. When the mats arrived on site for installation on an unusually cold day in December 2008, they were frozen and had to thaw before they could be unrolled. Despite these less-than-ideal conditions, the mats established well. They looked good during a visit six months later, and remained intact during use of the helipad.

Scientists at Columbia University in New York City have established several green roof research stations in different parts of the city. On one of these projects, a retrofit over an existing membrane on an old row house–style building near the center of the campus, light weight was imperative and access was difficult. Pregrown mats laid on 2 inches (5 cm) of medium simplified the installation process, and the weight of the assembly—12 pounds per square foot (58.6 kg per square meter) when saturated—is half that of another extensive roof monitored by the Columbia scientists.

Modules are trays, most often made of black plastic, con-

Lightweight mats were used to install this Columbia University retrofit project. The assembly weighs only 12 pounds per square foot (58.6 kg per square meter) when fully saturated. Photograph by Linda McIntyre

taining several inches of growing medium and plants. They are available prevegetated, with plants in place, and pregrown, with plants already established (the latter should always be specified if modules are used). Modules are laid out like pavers on the roof membrane and, though heavy, are considered relatively easy to move and replace.

Modules have been popular in North America, where uncertainty, fear, and skepticism of green roofs remain high, but they are virtually nonexistent in Germany, Switzerland, and other places with lots of green roofs. When owners or facilities managers are concerned about potential leaks or other problems with green roofs, modules are often considered a good compromise approach.

If modules are used on a green roof project, they should always be specified as "pregrown" rather than "prevegetated" to get the most benefit from offsite establishment.

Modules are usually, however, the most expensive way to plant a green roof. Customers pay for the establishment of plants off-site, and then they pay to transport the finished trays to the site and to get them on the roof, which can be a more difficult and time-consuming process than handling bulk growing medium and cuttings or plugs. Pregrown modules must be carefully handled during installation to avoid damage to plants and loss of growing medium from the trays. They should be picked up and carried, rather than dragged, across the roof to avoid damaging the waterproofing membrane.

Once they are installed, the convenience that drives the widespread use of modular systems often proves elusive. The trays are heavier than they might appear to be: a 4 square foot (0.4 square meter) module with 4 inches (10 cm) of growing medium and plants can weigh about 80 pounds (36.4 kg). On trays with a lip around the edge, the exposed plastic can degrade in sunlight, making moving them even more difficult. In addition, any gaps between the trays can compromise the waterproofing membrane by leaving it exposed in places and by allowing tree seedlings and other weeds to grow.

While little research has been done on the impact of design choices on green roof performance, some doubt the efficacy of modular systems for functions such as stormwater management.

Green roof modules are expensive to pack up and transport.

"I'm not sure modules are a green roof," says engineer and designer Charlie Miller. They function more like a series of miniature gardens, he says, or pots lined up on a roof. Edge effects—the tendency of the perimeter of the system to exhibit different conditions, in which plants are often drier and more stressed—are multiplied as the system is broken up into small discrete parts. "It's a way to get plants on the roof, but from an engineering standpoint, it's harder to get the benefits."

Sometimes, however, modules are the best or even the only way to install a green roof on a building. While the system itself is expensive, installation costs can be lower on small residential projects or on commercial projects where only passenger elevators or stairs can be used to transport materials. Innovations such as designs without exposed plastic edges and the use of biodegradable materials for the trays might improve their performance by more closely simulating an integral system functioning as a whole. Some plastic modules are designed with flush edges that also feature gaps through which roots can grow, and the grid of the biodegradable system disappears as the material breaks down. These approaches also improve the appearance of modular installations by eliminating the telltale plastic grid.

An effort by the Chesapeake Bay Foundation to mitigate the impact of stormwater in the Anacostia River watershed in the

Plants can become hot, dry, and stressed around the edges of plastic modules.

Washington, D.C., area was the impetus for a green roof project on the headquarters of the American Psychological Association. Then–vice president Skip Calvert met with Dawn Gifford of the green roof advocacy and consulting group DC Greenworks. Gifford helped secure funding from the TKF Foundation, which funds reflective spaces in the Baltimore-Washington region.

Cost was a big factor in this project, especially because the building did not need a new roof. But the availability of modules, which could be taken up the freight elevator and easily installed over the existing membrane without the need for heavy equipment, made it feasible. "We want to show people you can do this without spending a lot of money," says Nancy Kiefer of the World Resources Institute, which also has offices in the building and

Modules were the only way a green roof installation on the American Psychological Association headquarters was feasible.
Photograph by David Chester

was involved in the funding and logistics of the project. The building staff is considering adding additional green space.

The accessible roof features seating and a hardscape labyrinth, in addition to the 3000 square feet (297 square meters) of greened area. The labyrinth is an unusual and popular attraction, but both Kiefer and Mary Wyatt of the TKF Foundation think the green aspect is a big factor in the roof's heavy visitation. The plants make the roof more comfortable and pleasant in the Wash-

Biodegradable modules, such as these at the California Academy of Sciences, are installed like their plastic counterparts. Photograph courtesy of the SWA Group

The biodegradable modules quickly begin to break down, and eventually they disappear completely.

ington summer heat, and the accessibility and central location, close to Capitol Hill and the National Mall, makes this roof a great outreach tool.

The stylish and innovative green roof on San Francisco's California Academy of Sciences, rebuilt in 2008 after its predecessor was destroyed by the Loma Prieta earthquake, is unique, and a then-novel solution was developed to plant its celebrated domes. Typical green roof modules might have worked as a means to install plants on the steeply sloped domes in a stable fashion, but the black plastic grid look that characterizes some of these applications was completely at odds with this visible and high-style project. In addition, architect Renzo Piano wanted to avoid plastic plant containers to the fullest possible extent in the name of sustainability.

This conundrum, and Piano's desire for almost instant plant cover, prompted Paul Kephart, a restoration ecologist whose firm helped to develop a native plant palette for the roof, and a group of researchers to develop a biodegradable green roof module. The 289 square inch (1865 square centimeter) trays were made of coconut fiber, a waste product from coconut cultivation in the Philippines, held together with natural latex. They were filled with 3 inches (7.5 cm) of growing medium, treated with mycorrhizal fungi, and set on an additional 3 inches (7.5 cm) of medium spread out in the large squares delineated by a network of basalt stone gabions.

Plants were pregrown in the trays at Kephart's commercial nursery before being transported to the roof. Their biodegradability made it important to keep to the construction schedule so that the modules did not start to break down before being placed on the roof. Landscape architect John Loomis says the project's installation schedule pushed the life span of the trays to the limit. A few months after installation a small leak required that a few trays be removed for repair; the bottom of the trays had virtually disappeared, and the plants had developed 6-inch (15-cm) root systems. Kephart has gone on to use the biodegradable trays in other projects.

Non-green aspects of green roofs: loading, waterproofing, and drainage

However alive and attractive it is, a green roof is still a roof and has to provide all of a roof's typical functions. Designers and installers should be well versed in roof-related issues and construction details, including wind uplift; penetrations; clearance between pipes, walls, and curbs; and flashing. A good source of information on these subjects is the National Roofing Contractors Association's Vegetative Roof Systems Manual.

Structural considerations

The weight of any specific green roof depends on many variables, including the composition of the growing medium, the depth of the full green roof assembly, the materials used, the plant palette, and, most significantly, whether it will be supporting multiple people on a regular basis—that is, whether it was designed with usable space such as patios, decks, and walkways. While extensive green roofs are often thought of simply as stormwater management tools, they can be designed as attractive public spaces if the weight of such activity can be supported.

As with any roof, an accurate assessment of load-bearing capability is crucial on a green roof project, and it must be designed to accommodate both the stable dead load—the roofing components themselves as well as any mechanical equipment housed on the roof—and the variable live load, including people, furniture, maintenance equipment, rain, and snow. Construction loads associated with installation equipment should also be considered (NRCA 2009). Minimum structural requirements are dictated by local building codes.

Green roofs, with their layered structure and water-holding capabilities, weigh more than conventional roofs. Water alone weighs more than 8 pounds per gallon (0.96 kg per L) and about 62 pounds per cubic foot (993 kg per cubic meter; U.S. Geological Survey 2009), and many green roofs are designed to hold a high volume of stormwater. Water that is captured and held should be considered part of a green roof's dead load.

To make sure the assembly is not too heavy for the roof structure, green roof substrates should be specified by weight as well as depth. To make sure structural considerations are given the appropriate level of attention, a structural engineer should be part of the design team, and the designers and clients should insist that specifications for medium and other components be verified by a testing laboratory.

When fully saturated and with mature plant cover, the thinnest extensive green roofs weigh about 13 pounds per square foot (63.4 kg per square meter); more standard extensive roofs with 3 to 4 inches (7.5 to 10 cm) of growing medium weigh more, about 17 to 18 pounds per square foot (83 to 88 kg per square meter). Deeper intensive systems can weigh 35 pounds per square foot (170.8 kg per square meter) or much more. According to some estimates, most of the flat roofs on commercial buildings in North America can support up to about 25 pounds per square foot (122 kg per square meter), enough to accommodate a saturated green roof system with 3 to 4 inches (7.5 to 10 cm) of growing medium, though a building's structural capacity must be verified by a structural engineer before a green roof is installed as a retrofit.

Protocols for calculating the weight and dead load for green roofs are available from the ASTM International (E2397 and E2399) and should be used. If such testing is impossible, the insurance company Factory Mutual Global recommends calculating the dead load of saturated growing medium at a saturated weight of not less than 100 pounds per cubic foot (1601.8 kg per cubic meter) (Factory Mutual Global 2007).

Waterproofing

The first job of any roof, green or conventional, is to keep water out of the building. Waterproofing is an enormous and complex topic that we have neither the space nor the expertise to discuss in detail here. There are, however, some important points that everyone involved in a green roof project should consider when selecting a waterproofing membrane.

Make sure materials are appropriate for a green roof

Many types of waterproofing membrane are available, and all have their pluses and minuses. Offerings include built-up roofing, comprising alternating layers of felt and hot asphalt; modified bitumen, a blend of asphalt and polymer; single-ply sheets of plastic, PVC, rubber, or thermoplastic polyolefin; and various fluid-applied products.

The National Roofing Contractors Association (NRCA) recommends the following membrane types for green roof applications: nominal 215-mil (0.215-inch, 5.375-mm) minimum thickness, fabric reinforced, hot-fluid-applied, polymer-modified asphalt membrane; two-layer minimum APP- or SBS-polymer-modified bitumen sheet membrane; 60-mil (0.06-inch, 1.5-mm) minimum thickness reinforced EPDM membrane with stripped-in lap seams; or fabric-reinforced, one- or two-component, fluid-applied elastomeric membrane (Graham 2007).

Protect the membrane during installation

On a green roof project, a waterproofing membrane must be able to withstand the overburden of the green roof system without damage. The roots of green roof plants, as well as those of weeds or tree saplings that might show up on the roof, can damage some membranes. Some membrane materials naturally repel

It's imperative to protect the waterproofing membrane while the rest of the assembly is being installed. Loose nails or other equipment can cause leaks that might not be discovered until after the project is completed, when it's expensive and inconvenient to undertake repairs.

roots, whereas others will require a separate root barrier layer. Designers should check with the manufacturer for recommendations. The FLL guidelines also include methods for determining the root resistance of various waterproofing materials and installing root barriers when necessary (FLL 2008).

Some mats used for drainage and water retention, alone or in conjunction with other drainage materials, also provide protection for the membrane. In an inverted assembly, with insulation installed above the membrane, the insulation serves as a protective layer. Again, the best approach is to consult the membrane manufacturer's recommendations for protection materials.

The membrane's integrity must be preserved throughout the process of installing the green roof system. The typical phased construction schedule is difficult, because ideally the green roof is installed at the end of the process. A drainage course and the growth medium can provide some protection for the membrane, but temporary roofing overlaying the membrane, while somewhat costly, offers more protection and makes the need for expensive and time-consuming membrane replacement much less likely. Care should be taken, however, that the protection itself does not damage the membrane—sheets of plywood, for example, can cause check-shaped tears if too much weight is placed on the corners. The NRCA recommends asphaltic boards or sheets, extruded polystyrene boards, or PVC sheets for this purpose if compatible with other components in the assembly (NRCA 2009).

Test for leaks before completing the installation

After application, a membrane's waterproofing capability and integrity is tested either by temporarily blocking drains and flooding the roof with water or by electric field vector mapping (EFVM), in which the electrical conductivity of water is used to precisely locate even tiny leaks. A wire loop is installed around the perimeter of the membrane to establish the potential for an electrical current; during testing, any breach in the waterproofing membrane will show up as contact between the surfaces above and below the membrane, highlighting the location of the leak (Miller and Eichhorn 2003).

The use of EFVM or other electronic leak detection technology might help to mitigate concerns about removing the green

The membrane must be tested before the rest of the assembly is installed. An electronic leak detection system can be left in place and used after installation to locate leaks, making repair easier. Photograph courtesy of Furbish Company

roof overburden if a leak occurs, because the system remains in place and can be used after installation of the rest of the components. It isolates the leak area so that little material has to be removed during repairs, simplifying the process. EFVM technology can also be used on sloped roofs on which flood testing is difficult or impossible.

When properly designed and installed, the green roof assembly protects the membrane from the effects of heat and ultraviolet radiation. This protection and the potential longevity of the green roof assembly are undermined when the edges of the membrane are left exposed at the perimeter or around penetrations. Designers and installers should make sure the entire membrane is properly covered.

Drainage

Designing drainage on green roof projects is something of a balancing act, and a lot of variables, including the design intent of the project, regional climate and rainfall, the building's structural loading capacity, the roof's slope, and the desired plant palette, come into play. Like any roof, a green roof has to drain properly; the plumbing section of the local building code will provide design information about the minimum slope, number of drains, and other requirements (NRCA 2009).

There should never be standing water on a "flat" green roof—roofs that appear flat will almost always have a minimum slope of at least 0.25 inch per linear foot (2.1 cm per linear meter)—even during or after a major storm. Bad drainage adds weight to the roof, provides an unhealthy environment for most desirable plants, and risks degrading the growing medium (Miller 2008). At the same time, however, the green roof system has to hold enough water long enough to support healthy plants and, if stormwater management is a goal, to effectively reduce the volume of runoff and attenuate peak flows into sewer systems and receiving waters. When the green roof system reaches field capacity, it should drain like a conventional roof.

All flat roofs, unable to rely much on gravity to move water off the surface, have surface drains, subsurface pipes, gutters, downspouts, or other means to stay free of standing water. On a

Like all roofs, green roofs must drain properly. You should never see standing water on a green roof. Photograph courtesy of Tom Liptan

green roof, these mechanisms are still required to discharge water beyond the holding capacity of the system. Green roof assemblies that are built in place have a drainage layer, separated from the growing medium by a root-permeable filter fabric to prohibit the migration of small particles and debris, that promotes the movement of water from a saturated assembly into the roof's drainage system. Modules usually have drainage holes along the underside of the tray, and sometimes they are laid on other drainage materials as part of the full assembly. Some are also designed with channels on the underside to laterally move water across the roof.

In a green roof system built in place, the drainage layer usually consists of a course of drainage medium (a coarser, more freely draining aggregate than growing medium), synthetic sheets, or a combination of these elements. The sheets fall into two broad categories: those providing only drainage, and those that also retain some water in small depressions. Those providing retention look a bit like a large plastic egg carton, while drainage-only sheets can take a variety of forms: a tangle of polymer filaments, porous synthetic fabric, or foam boards with grooves or other surface formations to promote the movement of water (Wingfield 2005).

Each approach has advantages and disadvantages. Drainage aggregate usually holds more water and offers a hospitable horti-

Drainage aggregate (left) is coarser and more freely draining than growing medium (right).

cultural environment in which roots can spread and effectively take up water and nutrients, promoting healthy plants. Its performance can be adjusted by using different materials or particle sizes, and it can support any kind of irrigation system. In some climates drainage aggregate can offer superior performance at a lower cost (Gangnes 2007).

A granular course is usually heavier than sheets, but unless structural load restrictions are extremely tight, the weight difference for the overall system is often negligible. A granular layer's ability to hold water longer makes it ideal for stormwater management and most plant palettes. But it might be less suited to areas with high humidity, where it can take longer for the system to dry out and regain its ability to receive and retain stormwater.

Drainage sheets, boards, or mats are lighter than granular drainage medium. They can cost less, are easier and less labor-intensive than aggregate to install, and can be more transmissive, shedding water more quickly. Some systems—those with the egg-carton-like indentations, sometimes called retention sheets—are designed to hold some water for later uptake by plants. But the retention sheets' performance for this purpose is debatable. Water held in an indented plastic surface might not provide the same horticultural benefits as water distributed through an aggregate system through which roots can grow. In addition, the actual

Left: Some drainage sheets consist of soft synthetic fabrics, such as the ones beneath these layers of drainage aggregate and filter fabric.

Below: Other drainage sheets are more rigid and are designed with depressions to retain small amounts of water.

volume of water retained when the system is installed as recommended by the manufacturer is likely to be lower than the quoted volume for the sheets (Miller 2003).

Supplementing these kinds of retention sheets with a course of drainage medium can improve the system's horticultural capability, though this approach will add weight, complexity, and cost to the design. When system weight is of paramount concern (for example, on a retrofit with structural limitations) or when high transmissivity and a drier substrate is desirable (for example, in an area with high weed pressure), a sheet drainage approach can offer a good design solution.

When a green roof design includes paving, the designer should ensure that the drainage used underneath the pavers is appropriate. Some sheets lack the required compression strength and stability to support pavers (Weiler and Scholz-Barth 2009). Finally, the construction documents should make clear how to install sheets. On some projects retention sheets have been installed upside down, making it impossible for them to function as specified.

Moisture retention

Some green roof assemblies include a moisture retention layer of synthetic fabric underneath drainage boards with small cups or reservoirs, ostensibly to make additional water available to plants. The materials used and their characteristics vary, and little specialized research has been done on this component and its performance in the field, so it is difficult to assess the effectiveness of this approach.

Some designers find it helpful to use moisture retention mats underneath areas of medium that have been mounded to provide a deeper environment for plants in some areas of the roof, making a broader plant palette possible. The mats retain a bit of extra water and can help to stabilize the mounded area as the roots grow into the mat fabric.

The three-acre meadow atop Aquascapes headquarters in Illinois attracts birds and insects with native prairie grasses and perennials.

3 State of the Industry

Key Points

- The green roof industry is immature, and choosing among products and methods can be confusing.
- Use the guidelines, standards, and other sources of information that are available.
- Designers and specifiers should build a reliable supply chain. When you have control or input, vet your contractors and suppliers and visit facilities.
- Well-defined objectives, thoughtful design, clear assignment of responsibility, and continued engagement with the project will go a long way toward managing risks in a green roof project.
- Local policies can have an impact on your project. Applicable regulations and available incentives might make a green roof an attractive option.

The North American green roof industry is in its early stages. In the face of a growing but still small number of projects, few data from the field, and few objective standards, it can be difficult for a newcomer to sort through competing products and claims. Although there are many more extensive green roofs than there were a decade ago, the amount of green roof as a percentage of total roof area here is vanishingly small. Many North American green roofs are only a few thousand square feet (few hundred square meters), so economies of scale and pronounced public benefits have yet to materialize. But green roofs have become better known and more widely accepted in the public mind, perhaps because interest in environmental issues has increased in recent years, and this has drawn attention from all corners of the design, construction, horticultural, and landscape industries.

The recent surge in enthusiasm for green roof technology, however, has been a bit of a double-edged sword. As more vendors sell more products and more designers take on green roof projects, the expanded choices and additional experience *should* move the industry forward. And in many respects they are. But the good intentions behind most of these endeavors are not always enough to ensure successful projects. Any new technology, or any existing technology adapted to use in a different context, is going to entail a period of trial and error, and green roofs are no exception. The passion that often brings people into the industry sometimes backfires, resulting in inappropriate materials or ill-conceived designs. Eventually competition and the accumulation of data and experience will sort the market out. But in the meantime, while most people want to do the right thing with respect to green roofs, not everyone knows what the right thing is.

This will have to change if green roofs are to become a mainstream choice and a truly effective ecosystem service tool. The long-term health and growth of the industry depends on the availability of materials with consistent characteristics and performance that has been validated in the field. It also depends on the construction of enough projects to produce the needed data and experience.

The North American green roof industry is currently caught in something of a chicken-or-egg pattern. There are not yet enough green roofs in this part of the world to prove conclusively the reliability and performance of the technology and establish economies of scale, bringing down costs for materials and installation. But without proven reliability and performance and economies of scale, it is more difficult to reach that critical mass. Many of those who have led the industry up to this point are driven by a passionate belief in the potential for green roofs to significantly improve the built environment. Passion alone, however, is not enough. The green roof industry will have to move to the next level and prove that it can build projects on a large scale at a reasonable cost that perform successfully and predictably.

Buyer beware

The most disadvantaged party in the marketplace as it now stands is the consumer. If you want to buy a car or refrigerator, you can easily find a lot of objective information about the performance and reliability of different models and guidelines on how much you should expect to pay. If you want to put a green roof on your house or commercial building, however, there are few independent resources or disinterested opinions available to objectively frame your choices. Adding insult to injury, prices for materials, especially growing medium, and labor are much higher in North America than in places, such as Germany, that have well-established green roof markets (Philippi 2006).

High prices, however, are not necessarily signifiers of quality. In the absence of widespread independent testing and certification, products with better or more aggressive marketing behind them can potentially crowd out products with better attributes. Nor are the difficulties limited to components. Some market participants bring expertise from related but discrete industries, such as roofing, nursery soils, or landscape installation, that might not transfer directly to green roofs without experience and careful analysis over time. Some tout credentials obtained by

In countries such as Germany, with well-established green roof industries, competition helps keep prices down. So does a sophisticated market in recycled building materials, some of which are used in growing medium.

purchasing study materials and taking tests but have little or no experience in the field. Some want to corner the green roof market, believing that their industry alone is uniquely qualified to design, build, and maintain green roofs.

But just as a green roof is a multifaceted creature—part of the building, yes, but also a living thing, a landscape built in part with engineered materials—no single industry or profession has all of the answers. Knowledge of roofing, plants, architecture, stormwater management, or other subjects is necessary but not always sufficient for a successful green roof project. An architect, a consultant, a landscape architect, a roofer, an engineer, or a combination of such individuals might be able to design and build your desired green roof. But a different architect, consultant, landscape architect, roofer, or engineer might be ill-equipped to handle the job.

Manufacturers or sellers of components might have engineered innovative solutions that help promote healthy, stable, long-lived green roofs. But asserting quality does not guarantee it. Components should be tested, and providers of medium and plants must keep their sites and products free of contaminants such as weed seeds. Designers who specify components should exercise due diligence rather than relying on brochures, websites, or sales pitches.

It's important for designers to vet their suppliers carefully in the absence of established industry standards for components.

In such a marketplace, the buyer must beware. On the upside, things are getting better. Ongoing research can inform product use and development as well as design. Built projects, even (or especially) failed ones, are adding to the body of green roof knowledge. And even now there are some tools available to help inform green roof design and installation decisions.

In light of this state of affairs, it is reasonable—and imperative to the maturation of the industry—for the building owner or client to hold designers and installers to a high standard. Designers and installers, in turn, should vet their suppliers and the materials they provide for quality and consistency.

Criteria for success should be defined early in the design phase, and the project at completion and afterward should be measured against these criteria. Problems might arise, but careful planning based on realistic objectives, as well as not trying to reinvent the wheel, can forestall many of them. Others can be avoided by the selection of an experienced team qualified to handle difficulties that crop up on site, and yet others can be mitigated by continued engagement after installation.

Guidelines and standards

The most comprehensive and detailed green roof information currently available is compiled in the guidelines developed in Germany by the Landscape Research, Development, and Construction Society, known by its German initials FLL (for Forschungsgesellschaft Landschaftsentwicklung Landschaftsbau). The society's green roof working group has been developing and refining standards and specifications for green roof growing medium, construction methods and materials, and planting information for more than twenty-five years. In addition to basic green roof information and the relatively well-known standards for growing and drainage media, the guidelines address a broad range of issues such as the relationship between site conditions and plant choice and technical issues such as slope and loading. They do not, however, recommend specific products or plants (Philippi 2005).

An English version of the FLL Guidelines for the Planning,

Execution, and Upkeep of Green Roof Sites can be purchased online. These guidelines have provided critical guidance on many early green roof projects in North America. Many pioneers here learned about green roofs in Germany and successfully adapted German extensive green roof technology here. This approach has worked especially well in the Northeast, mid-Atlantic, and Great Lakes regions of the United States, but the guidelines do include some flexibility to help adapt them to a range of climates.

Some FLL-compliant green roof components, such as growing medium, are available in North America, and testing of growing medium against the FLL guidelines with the same methodology is available from Penn State University. Testing is also available from other labs, but not all of them use methodology, such as compacting the medium with a proctor hammer, that will produce comparable results, and not all of them have the frame of reference to analyze the unique properties required by green roof systems (Penn State University Agriculture Analytic Services Lab, no date).

U.S.-based ASTM International has also established a green roof task force and recently published a series of testing methodologies and broad guidelines for plant selection, installation, and maintenance (ASTM International 2009). The group's sustainability subcommittee is also working on a Guide for Green Roof Systems to identify relevant terminology, principles, and concepts as well as a more ambitious Practice for Assessment of Green Roofs (ASTM International 2007).

The insurance company Factory Mutual Global publishes loss prevention recommendations for green roofs that can help guide design and assist in the selection of components (Factory Mutual Global 2007). The document includes useful discussions of important issues including loading and wind resistance. The company also publishes a separate document on designing to compensate for wind loads and recommendations for the waterproofing membrane and below-membrane components.

Standards, while immensely helpful, are not a magic solution. You still have to do your homework. Selecting the best components for specific objectives still requires analysis and often guesswork. Both the European and the U.S. markets lack standards for most synthetic products. Green roof engineer and designer Charlie Miller, who has been active in ASTM's green roof task force, cites the following wish list of new performance tests for materials: media capillarity; fabric capillarity; puncture resistance under conditions relevant to green roofs; drainage capacity based on testing of integrated drainage systems; and root permeability of fabrics.

Furthermore, guidelines and design standards are only as good as the specifications derived from them. In the design process, broad statements making a reference to compliance with a standard are insufficient without specification of the details necessary to satisfy the standard. Neglecting to do so can leave contractors without enough information to properly price bids, result in change orders during the construction process, or leave the client dissatisfied with the completed project (D'Annunzio 2003).

Research and testing

Over the past decade, research at universities such as Penn State, North Carolina State, Michigan State, Columbia, University of Toronto, Southern Illinois University-Edwardsville, Oregon State University, and others has made an invaluable contribution to the body of green roof knowledge. To name just a few achievements, scientists and students have validated the ability of green roofs to help manage stormwater runoff (for example, EPA 2009a), compared plant species' ability to survive on a rooftop environment (Monterusso et al. 2005), and analyzed the potential for green roofs to reduce the urban heat island effect (Rosenzweig et al. 2006) and to make a modest contribution to carbon sequestration (Getter et al. 2009).

Yet more remains to be done. The data on stormwater quantity are strong, but those on peak flow reduction and transient retention are not as good. More data are needed on the effects of scale, that is, how the performance of a roof measured in acres (hectares) differs from that of a small roof of a few thousand square feet (few hundred square meters). Many of the products and materials used in green roofs have no performance data associated with them, so they should be monitored and analyzed, especially in conjunction with other products and materials in a full green roof system. Among the most glaring gaps is the lack of long-term data—most studies have analyzed timeframes of three years or (usually) less. Long-term data will enable more precise design, and monitoring multiple sites would enable the direct comparison of different design approaches, both among different green roofs and with respect to diverse arrays of green infrastructure (Traver 2009).

Research that further confirms and quantifies the benefits of green roofs and that sheds light on how to design green roofs to maximize the desired benefits is likely to increase the number of built projects. The data will give governments the information they need to establish policies and incentives that help them deal

Academic research has provided valuable green roof data, but more needs to be done. At Oregon State University, researchers are testing different plant species and analyzing runoff from various assemblies.

with municipal problems such as water quality impairments from stormwater runoff. Those incentives will make green roofs more economical to install. Stronger, more detailed quantification of benefits will also reassure building owners that green roofs are a functional and mainstream building option worthy of routine consideration. Better tools to measure the performance of different materials will make the marketplace less of a minefield and take some of the guesswork out of the specification process.

Professional and industry information

With many professions and industries vying for pieces of the green roof pie, various groups and even some individual companies have moved to position themselves as leaders in green roof design and installation. No one profession is uniquely suited to green roof design and installation, and there is no typical composition of a green roof project team. Teams comprising individuals with many different backgrounds, including architecture, landscape architecture and design, engineering, roofing, horticulture, and more have designed and installed successful green roofs. Experience, continued engagement with finished projects, and a willingness to correct and learn from mistakes will be the best guides.

While some of these campaigns are simply predictable marketing efforts, in some cases useful and free information is available to the public. Local chapters of professional associations can help locate individuals and firms with green roof project experience.

Green Roofs for Healthy Cities

The industry trade group Green Roofs for Healthy Cities, based in Toronto, holds an annual conference including an award program for green roof projects. Information about award winners, along with some general information about green roofs and advertisements for member companies, can be viewed on the group's website. The group also sells educational materials and recently established an accreditation program based on a written examination.

American Society of Landscape Architects

In 2006 the American Society of Landscape Architects (ASLA) had a green roof installed on its headquarters in Washington, D.C. The roof, with an exuberant and complex design unlikely to be replicated, was conceived as a demonstration project. It is open for public visits and tours, and the group provides information about the project on its website. Many people, including landscape architects, other designers, government officials, and curious environmentalists have visited the roof since its official open-

The green roof on the American Society of Landscape Architects headquarters building, with its flamboyant waves of vegetation, has drawn a lot of attention.

ing, and the high-profile project has done much to promote green roofs in the city.

The ASLA has offered green roof tours and education sessions at its annual conferences, and provides some broad general information about green roofs and other sustainable design measures on its website. Some green roof project information associated with recipients of its annual design awards is also available.

American Institute of Architects

The American Institute of Architects (AIA) has a practice group, the Committee on the Environment, for members interested in sustainable design. For more than a decade, the Committee has presented annual awards to its "Top Ten Green Projects," highlighting innovative designs including those using green roofs. Information about winning projects, including selection criteria, is available online. The AIA also provides general information about green building on its website, including resources for potential clients, but there is little information or technical guidance specific to green roofs.

National Roofing Contractors Association

Green roofs are still a small slice of the total roofing pie. Some roofers have developed a sideline in green roofs, others hope to capitalize on the growing interest, and still others remain skeptical. The National Roofing Contractors Association (NRCA) has established a Center for Environmental Innovation in Roofing to provide members and others with information about more ecologically friendly roofing choices, including green roofs; to encourage and publicize research; and to expand market opportunities. In addition, the NRCA publishes a Vegetative Roof Systems Manual, including useful construction details, descriptions of components, and best practices for green roof design and installation from the roofing perspective.

Manufacturers

Some manufacturers of roofing materials also offer technical information, specifications, or educational materials, even online courses, free of charge. This kind of information varies widely in quality and usefulness. Members of professional groups can in some cases satisfy continuing education credits with this kind of course, but it can also be useful for those who simply want to learn more about green roof technology.

Design and installation firms

Some firms with a specialty in green roofs provide detailed technical and project information on their websites. It is worth exploring the websites of experienced firms for such information, even if you cannot hire those firms for your project. Identifying and, when possible, visiting similar projects can provide a wealth of information to designers and owners.

Risk assessment

Because a green roof is still a relatively new concept in North America, perceptions of the risks associated with them can be a bit skewed and sometimes overblown. Designing and installing an extensive green roof should usually be a straightforward process, and averting risks with a green roof is best done in the same way as on any construction project. Clarify your objectives early. Define expectations in a realistic manner. Design to meet those objectives and expectations. Clearly define areas of responsibility to ensure the integrity of the design through the installation process and after occupancy. Address any postinstallation problems early and head on. Assign clear responsibility and instructions for maintenance during the establishment period and over the long term.

But until green roofs become more widely accepted—something industry players can promote by taking responsibility for the performance of their projects—heavy reliance on managing risks, real and exaggerated, will probably continue to dampen demand and drive the use of methods (proprietary systems and modules) that might not be the best or most cost-effective means to meeting a building owner's objectives.

Warranties

Most green roof fears are associated with potential leaks. This is the case even though a properly installed green roof system, like an inverted roof membrane assembly, protects the waterproofing membrane from the degrading effects of heat, temperature fluctuation, and sunlight, the three main causes of membrane failure. A properly selected, installed, and tested membrane under a green roof assembly (see "Waterproofing" in chapter 2) that was protected during the construction process should not leak. In fact, much of the reluctance to use green roof technology is based on the prevalence of badly installed, and therefore defective, *conventional* roofs (Weiler and Scholz-Barth 2009).

One way that fear of leakage is assuaged is through the use of a warranty covering the waterproofing membrane. But building owners should avoid putting too much faith in a long-term warranty to guarantee performance. Even the NRCA notes the deficiencies of such an approach. The warrantor's liability is often much more limited and exclusions more extensive than a consumer might assume, often rendering the warranty of little value in the case of leakage. Some companies have used warranties as marketing tools, and warranties tend to make owners complacent about proper specification and installation as well as their own responsibility for long-term maintenance (NRCA, no date). The NRCA recommends that consumers base their decisions on objective analysis of proven options that can best serve their specific project requirements.

In green roof construction, the warranty issue is further complicated by the need to remove the overburden—the green roof system above the membrane—to fix any leaks that might arise, and to replace it after the repair is finished. Often the warranty for the membrane specifies that the manufacturer is not responsible for overburden removal and replacement, or the manufacturer will only provide this service if its own proprietary green roof system is used.

In the current green roof marketplace, the use and specification of such systems is sometimes substituted for analysis and specification of the best components for a project. These systems simplify the specification process for architects, and the warranty offers assurance for the owner, especially when phases of a project cannot always be staged in a manner that protects the membrane from damage caused by other tradespeople. But selecting and specifying the best components for the project's objectives, including the waterproofing membrane; making all tradespeople aware of the need to protect the membrane during construction and taking effective measures to do so; confirming the integrity of the membrane with EFVM or a flood test prior to the installation of the green roof system; and negotiating an appropriate warranty with the installer is the best way to build a successful green roof. An EFVM system, which is left in place and can be used to locate leaks even well after the installation of the green roof assembly (see "Waterproofing" in chapter 2), might also help to mitigate concern about leaks on all sides.

Finally, with respect to warranties, it is worth remembering that their terms are rarely set in stone. The owner must clarify, at the outset, the exact terms of the warranty and which aspects of the project are warranted and if so, by whom. In some cases, especially some proprietary systems, warranties are built into the purchase price, whereas in other cases warranties for different aspects of the assembly (such as plants) must be purchased separately. Sometimes manufacturers and installers are willing to negotiate terms that are different than their usual approach. These opportunities for flexibility, however, are rarely presented to those who do not ask.

Insurance

Recent developments in the insurance industry might help to put the risks associated with green roofs into some perspective. Many in the industry are concerned about the risks posed by the environmental impacts of climate change, and they see more sustainable building practices as a way to help mitigate those risks. "We rely on historical data to assess risk," says Stephen Bushnell of Fireman's Fund in the San Francisco Bay area. "But if the climate is changing, increasing the frequency and severity of hurricanes, wildfires, spring storms, and so on, that's not factored into the data."

Insurance companies including Fireman's Fund, CNA, and Lexington have established programs through which insured parties can repair or replace damaged property with sustainable materials and processes, including green roofs (Harrington 2008; CNA 2009; Ortega-Wells 2009). Coverage is also available to restore an insured building to an equal level or one level higher of LEED certification following a loss (Harrington 2008). Programs such as these and similar programs increasingly available to homeowners are likely to help bring sustainable building methods, including green roofs, into the mainstream and reinforce the advantages of using these methods. Bushnell says green buildings are better risks and safer for their occupants. Building owners have shown a similar enthusiasm; he says Fireman's Fund's green business doubled from 2007 to 2008.

Still, the full-scale greening of insurance will not be a speedy process. The growing, but still relatively small, number of green buildings does not yet confer actuarial credibility. Green roofs in particular pose an insurance challenge because failures associated with roofs, along with windows and doors, are where insurers see significant loss activity. Retrofits are of particular concern, says Bushnell: "Can the building support the weight of the roof, especially when the soil is saturated? Were the right materials used? Does the contractor know what he is doing? Does the contractor have insurance at adequate limits should the roof fail?"

Liability in the case of such failures usually rests squarely on designers and installers. For the owner, however, a lawsuit is a cumbersome undertaking that does not quickly or directly solve the problem. A more standardized and performance-based green roof industry would help address these concerns, making it possible for designers and installers to mitigate their own risk exposure.

Owners should also pay special attention to maintenance. Bushnell says that the way buildings, including green buildings, are operated and maintained has a significant effect on performance. Attention to the performance of green buildings is increasing, and some lawyers predict there will be lawsuits based on failure to live up to performance claims (Buckley 2009).

Some potential risks associated with green roofs, however, are more remote than others. Fire, for example, is often mentioned as a concern (Willoughby 2008) even though such discussions tend to be purely hypothetical—rarely do they focus on an actual fire event on a green roof. Proper design, including the use of appropriate growing medium and plants, and regular maintenance should address concerns about fire. In Germany, green roofs are considered to be fire-resistant if built and maintained according to FLL guidelines.

Third-party certification

These days it can seem as if virtually every new building project in the United States is seeking Leadership in Energy and Environmental Design (LEED) certification. LEED is a system developed by the U.S. Green Building Council (USGBC) for evaluating buildings based on site sustainability, water efficiency, energy use and impact on the atmosphere, materials and resources, indoor environmental quality, and design innovation. Points are allocated in each category and ratings include Certified, Silver, Gold, and Platinum, depending on the number of points accrued. Separate programs have been developed for different building types including schools, houses, and commercial buildings. The USGBC recently spun off a separate Green Building Certification Institute to run an accreditation program for designers and other green building professionals (see below) as well as the certification process.

Other certification programs to reward sustainability and energy efficiency exist, such as Green Globes in Canada and Energy Star for Buildings and Manufacturing Plants developed by the U.S. government. But LEED currently dominates the American building certification market, and despite some concerns about its suitability for such uses (Cheatham 2009a), the program is becoming embedded into codes, incentives, and other policies at the federal, state, and local levels (USGBC 2009).

The LEED program has endured some criticism for the high

cost and cumbersome nature of its certification process and for the difficulty of factoring regional considerations into the system (Schendler and Udall 2005; Kamenetz 2007). But by establishing clear (if broad) criteria, providing objective third-party certification at a time when interest in green building was growing rapidly, and expanding the market for sustainable design, LEED has changed the sustainable construction game, for which it deserves great credit. The USGBC has also made and continues to make efforts to improve and strengthen both the building certification and professional accreditation processes.

Green roof designers, installers, and others trying to navigate through the bewildering array of products and services on offer, however, will find no guidance from the program, either with respect to the products themselves or in terms of reference values for specification. Although it is billed as a performance-based system, LEED does not currently assess the actual performance of either green building projects once built or the components of systems such as green roofs, though USGBC appears to be taking some steps to move the program in that direction (Post 2009). Accreditation of one or more members of the project team does not necessarily mean that the individual or group has knowledge or experience that is directly relevant to your project.

A green roof is likely to earn a project points toward LEED certification in one or more categories, but achieving certification does not necessarily mean that the roof was properly designed and installed. Including a green roof in a project merely to earn LEED points can be a disservice to the building owner if there is no clearly defined objective for the roof.

This green roof sits on a LEED Platinum building, but the medium specification was clearly inappropriate, and its depth was insufficient to support the specified plants.

Accreditation

The USGBC's LEED program includes accreditation of professionals known as LEED APs. In 2009 the Green Building Certification Institute, which administers the program, updated it, making the accreditation process more rigorous and establishing requirements for continuing education in an effort to improve the program and comply with ISO 17024, the international standard for personnel certification (Roberts 2009). Previously, aspiring LEED APs had only to pass an 80-question computerized exam, something many were able to do relatively easily without either project experience or knowledge of architecture, design, or construction, with simply a few weeks of studying (for example, Posner 2008).

Now a range of LEED AP credentials are available. For those seeking LEED expertise for a project team, the most relevant under the new system will likely be the LEED AP+ category, which applies to professionals who have passed a specialist exam (for example, building design and construction or operations and maintenance) as well as the core exam. In addition to the tests, applicants for these credentials are required to have documented experience on at least one recent LEED project. A Green Associate category, similar to the former LEED AP program but with continuing education requirements, is available for less-experienced applicants such as students or marketing specialists. Those who earned accreditation under the former system will be integrated into a new category based on their experience and are subject to continuing education requirements (Roberts 2009).

The Toronto-based industry membership association Green Roofs for Healthy Cities has also recently launched an accreditation program. Aspiring green roof professionals can purchase preparatory courses and study guides from the group and sit for a 100-question exam. Keeping the credential current requires completion of continuing education sessions, at least half of which must be purchased from the group.

Don't rely too heavily on credentials

All of these credentials demonstrate that the holder has an interest in green building and a willingness to invest time, effort, and money to learn about it. But credentials alone cannot qualify an individual to play a particular role on a project as complex as a green roof. Even the most rigorous coursework, without an apprenticeship or practicum in the field, is unlikely on its own to fully prepare a person for a significant role on a project. And many knowledgeable and experienced green roof designers and installers have not pursued any kind of accreditation.

For those seeking employment in the green roof industry, accreditation offers no guarantee they will find it. While successful candidates for the LEED AP+ accreditations can go on to get jobs associated with the LEED documentation and certification processes, there is no particular profession associated with green roof design, installation, or maintenance. Architects, landscape architects, engineers, roofers, and others have built successful green roofs, but no profession has cornered the market. In Germany, which has a competitive and mature green roof market, there is no professional green roof certification.

Those seeking a green roof designer or installer in the North American market should look to a track record of successful projects as the most reliable indicator of competence. Complex or specific design objectives, such as stormwater management or wildlife habitat, will require additional special expertise. Professionals considering pursuing such credentials should also understand that earning and using those credentials might hold them to a higher standard of care if litigation arises out of projects that fail outright or fail to meet clients' expectations of certification or performance (Victor O. Schinnerer & Company, Inc. 2009). This theory is the subject of debate and has yet to be tested in the courts.

Green roof economics and the role of incentives

One of the most significant obstacles to green roof construction is the higher up-front cost of a green roof compared to a conventional flat black roof, or even compared to other sustainable strategies such as reflective white roofs, which when clean can save impressive amounts of energy (Rosenzweig et al. 2006). Even in established markets it's difficult to quantify benefits, and therefore return on investment, with any precision. "There have been many studies in Germany on whether a green roof pays off or not, and they all say that in the long run, including maintenance costs, it does," says green roof consultant Peter Philippi, who worked for years in Germany before establishing a business in the United States. "It is always on the positive side. It's just difficult to give a hard number." While these early "first costs" of green roofs are usually higher, proper valuation of the public as well as private benefits of green roofs, especially in urban areas, can mean that choosing a green roof makes sense and even saves money over the long term (Clark et al. 2008; MacMullen et al. 2008).

Integrating these public benefits, including stormwater management, reduction of the urban heat island effect, and mitigation of some forms of air pollution, into policy by the establishment of incentives for green roof construction could bring costs down, in effect monetizing those benefits. Lower costs would add to the body of experience and data in the industry, providing a clearer picture of what works best where and contributing to the establishment of best practices in design, installation, and maintenance. More data and experience would help municipal and regional authorities establish programs designed to meet their particular needs (for example, capturing stormwater for reuse in areas where the water supply is restricted).

LEED certification is popular because many owners and developers believe green buildings are good business in terms of performance, longevity, and perhaps especially marketing. There is a long way to go before the magnitude of these perceived benefits can be conclusively established and quantified. But these perceptions are functioning as de facto incentives for green development and retrofitting, accelerating the growth of the green construction sector even during the economic downturn (Ortega-Wells 2009).

Explicit incentives make it easier for building owners to calculate the return on their green roof investment. Many cities in North America, including Chicago; Portland, Oregon; Philadelphia; New York; Toronto; and Washington, D.C., have established incentives to promote green roof construction. While they vary from city to city and evolve frequently, available benefits include floor area ratio bonuses, expedited permitting, credits or abatements of taxes or stormwater fees, and grants. These programs can also help spread green building knowledge throughout the development community. San Francisco, for example, brought in private-sector employees to work on its green permit program. This has made the program more effective, and it's also a good way for local professionals to develop specialized green building experience (AIA 2008). Some local governments are going beyond incentives. In 2009 Toronto became the first city in North America to require a percentage of roof vegetation for large new construction projects.

It is too early to assess at this stage which array of incentives is most effective for promoting green roof construction. Tax abatement is a flexible approach that can provide an immediate payback for benefits that are otherwise realized over the longer term. Density bonuses are attractive in built-out cities and easy to quantify, as are grants. Expedited permitting can save owners and developers a lot of money, but the permitting authority must have the manpower and knowledge to make such a program work (AIA 2008). Toronto's bold move toward mandates might generate a backlash or desultory minimal compliance, but it might also lead to a critical mass of green roof area, a more competitive and efficient local industry, and innovative new design approaches.

Integrating green roofs into regulations and policy

Stormwater management regulations have driven a lot of North American green roof construction over the last decade. This is likely to continue as less funding is available for more traditional infrastructure controls and skepticism of their ability to deliver water quality improvements grows (Slone and Evans 2003; National Research Council 2008). But stormwater codes alone are probably insufficient to really bring green roofs into the development mainstream.

To effectively promote green roofs, or any other particular green infrastructure practice, integrating the practice into stormwater regulations is only the first step, says environmental scientist and policy analyst Chris Kloss. Greening goals are best realized when they are promoted with incentives and integrated with other policy frameworks such as zoning requirements. Kloss cites as an example a project he worked on involving ambitious volume-based stormwater controls in an urban watershed. "What came out of that was a lot of rainwater harvesting," he says. "Which is great. But to really green the city, you need an integrated complementary approach." This requires identification of priorities and refinement of goals. In some areas, reducing potable water use is a priority, whereas in others reducing the urban heat island effect might be more important. Municipal governments can work toward such goals through targeted incentives that might complement stormwater management objectives. They can also lead by example.

Lessons from three cities known for green roof promotion and construction are instructive. All are working to control CSOs and integrate green infrastructure into their stormwater regulations, but each has taken a different approach tailored to their various political climates, using incentives, regulations, and mandates in varying combinations.

Chicago: exercising, then codifying, political will

Chicago is synonymous with urban green roof construction in the minds of many, even outside the design field. After a European trip in 1998 sparked his interest in green roofs, Mayor Richard Daley engaged in a one-man campaign to green the city's rooftops. He started with his own at City Hall, a 20,000 square foot (1860 square meter) project first planted in 2000, when few in North America had even heard of green roofs. In 2003 the city's Department of Planning and Development held a series of seminars with the Chicago chapter of the Urban Land Institute to educate developers about green roofs, dispel fears and misconceptions about the technology, and determine which incentives would be most attractive.

Green roofs are now central components of the city's effective sustainable development policy, which is increasingly broad and also promotes, among other things, tree planting and greener streets and alleys. Specific green commitments (including, in many cases, planting of part or all of the available roof area) are required of all projects receiving financial or zoning assistance from the city. City buildings are also required to be LEED certified and to have green roofs whenever feasible. Incentives are available, too: Permits for green projects are expedited, green roofs count as pervious area in the calculation of stormwater retention requirements, and accessible green roofs are credited toward the open space impact fee on multifamily residential projects.

This leadership through force of personality—Daley frequently says he wants to make Chicago the greenest city in America—has gotten results, including about 600 green roof projects comprising almost 7 million square feet (651,000 square meters) of green roof. Living with these green roofs has convinced the city government that they work, reducing CSOs, saving energy, helping to mitigate the urban heat island effect, and improving quality of life in the city. Officials and staff are working to build a lasting sustainable policy framework embedded in

Chicago Mayor Richard Daley's green roof campaign started close to home, on the roof of City Hall.

local laws, with green roofs as a key element. With so much infrastructure already in place, the city is well positioned to move, as the Daley administration wishes to do, to a more performance-based system of requirements. Michael Berkshire, the green projects administrator in the city's Department of Planning and Development, says that with a critical mass of green roofs, they can consider policy changes such as a minimum set of specifications and a maintenance requirement in light of existing data. He and his colleagues will also be drawing on the local expertise that has grown along with the industry.

Berkshire believes the development community is starting to buy into the mayor's vision. Zoning lawyers and developers with whom he used to spar have mostly accepted green building and in some cases see it as the new normal. One developer told him recently that if a building is not LEED certified, it's obsolete when the doors open. "I've been waiting years to hear that," he says.

Portland, Oregon: an incentive-based green roof program as part of a multifaceted approach to stormwater management

Portland, Oregon, with its outdoorsy, activist culture, has been a leader in promoting green infrastructure, including green roofs (known locally as ecoroofs, because unirrigated roofs might not be very green during the city's dry summers). Portland's ecoroof program grew out of a broader effort started in 1991 to better manage CSOs, which had been discharging 6 billion gallons (22.8 billion L) of untreated wastewater and stormwater into the Columbia Slough and Willamette River every year. Part of the program's genesis was a lawsuit under the Clean Water Act, after which the EPA required the city to implement stricter stormwater controls (City of Portland, Bureau of Environmental Services [CoPBES] 2009a).

The city sought to respond with a program of green infrastructure, but the EPA would not at that point sign off on such an approach. Portland is nearing completion of a $1.4 billion pair of big pipes that were designed to satisfy that mandate. But it also went ahead with a slate of green infrastructure measures anyway, uniting ecology-based and traditional programs in a combined "Grey to Green" initiative designed by Sam Adams, a former Bureau of Environmental Services commissioner who became Portland's mayor in 2009. Ecoroofs are a significant part of that effort, along with the city's award-winning Green Streets program, tree planting, and other sustainable stormwater controls.

Portland began building ecoroof demonstration projects in the 1990s and recognized them as a stormwater best management practice (regulations require on-site management of runoff) in 1999. Technical and permitting assistance from its Bureau of Environmental Services, along with public meetings and outreach, helped to foster acceptance in the development community. A grant component in its green building program and a popular density bonus pegged to the percentage of ecoroof coverage were established in 2001 (Liptan 2003).

Building on this progress, in 2008 Portland set a goal of building an additional 43 acres (17.2 ha) of ecoroof in five years.

Portland has a city policy of installing green roofs on any city building roof that needs replacement, unless structural or other problems make it economically unfeasible.

"We wanted to build momentum, start to demonstrate benefits, and generate information to share," says Lisa Libby, the mayor's planning and sustainability director. "The goal is ambitious, but relatively modest compared to the total roof area of the city," about 12,500 acres (5000 ha; Bingham 2009). To help achieve the goal, an ecoroof-specific grant program that provides up to $5 per square foot for ecoroof projects was established. Grants were requested for more than fifty projects, both commercial and residential, in the first year of the program. Some in the design industry have noted that the grant effectively halves the price per square foot of a basic ecoroof assembly (King 2009).

Portland's leaders are aggressively using incentives to encourage private actions that take some of the pressure off the conveyance system, such as downspout disconnection for both residential and commercial sewer ratepayers. Disconnecting downspouts alone is keeping more than 1 billion gallons (3.8 billion L) of runoff out of the sewer system every year (CoPBES 2009a). Other cities are starting to take note of Portland's efforts, which are expected to reduce CSO volume by 96 percent by 2011 (CoPBES 2009b).

Similarly, Portland has used a light touch to promote and build public support for ecoroof construction. The city relies almost entirely on incentives and currently requires few design details from those seeking support for ecoroof projects. But the program continues to evolve, informed by experience and the accrual of data. Tom Liptan, an ecoroof pioneer (he built the city's first ecoroof on his garage in 1996) and landscape architect with the Bureau of Environmental Services, which administers the grants, says that the program is structured so that the agency can direct resources to projects most likely to perform well. For example, a system with 4 inches (10 cm) of medium is preferred for stormwater performance, but buildings being retrofit with ecoroofs might lack the structural capacity for such a system, so they are not required to meet that standard. So far, Liptan says requests and available funds have matched up quite well, so grants have been available to most everyone who requests them. But interest is clearly growing, so the program is likely to become more competitive.

Philadelphia: thinking at the watershed level and raising the bar for performance

Philadelphia, situated between two rivers and with a long tradition of community greening, has been at the forefront of innovative stormwater management solutions using green infrastructure. In 1999 the city's water department integrated its CSO, stormwater management, and source water protection programs under the auspices of a newly established an Office of Watersheds to better identify potential controls and implement effective long-term improvements (Philadelphia Water Department 2009). A 2006 stormwater manual update emphasized integrated site design and reductions in impervious cover to advance the goal of controlling the first inch of rainfall on new development sites. The manual also set out detailed design, materials, and maintenance recommendations for green roofs.

According to Glen Abrams, a planner in the Office of Watersheds, the approach represents an effort to move green roofs toward better performance. While at this time the office is counting green roofs designed according the manual (at least 3 inches [7.5 cm] of medium with characteristics in line with FLL guidelines and ASTM testing methods) as pervious surface area for the purpose of stormwater management requirements, the manual does acknowledge that green roofs are not zero-discharge systems and it requires site designs to accommodate runoff. If new information indicates that green roofs are more effective or less effective at controlling runoff, the requirements and credits could change in either direction.

Philadelphia is in a good position to serve as a laboratory of green roof performance. The city benefits from the proximity of a dynamic design community including green roof and general design firms and academic programs focused on both research and design. A growing number of built projects and continued analysis of data on stormwater and other performance metrics will inform the development of policy.

In the meantime, green roof construction in the city is becoming more attractive. A move toward a parcel-based billing system for stormwater fees might mean significant monthly savings for some ratepayers with green roofs. Starting in 2010, owners of commercial, industrial, and institutional properties or multifamily residential buildings will pay a gross area charge based on size of parcel, plus an impervious area charge that could have a large impact on the amount of the fee. The new system, however, will include a credit that will benefit properties that meet the criteria set out in the stormwater manual, including those with green roofs.

Beyond stormwater policy, the city recently established a tax incentive for private-sector projects in the form of a credit against their business privilege tax for 25 percent of the cost of green roof installation (up to $100,000). It applies to green roofs that comprise 50 percent of total roof area or 75 percent of eligible roof area, whichever is greater. Abrams says that this, along with re-

PECO, Philadelphia's electric and gas utility company, was able to take advantage of a new tax incentive when the company installed its green roof in late 2008. Photograph courtesy of Roofscapes

duced stormwater fees and projected savings on roof replacement, energy costs, and other green roof benefits, could make green roofs an increasingly attractive and economical choice for owners and developers in Philadelphia.

Your local, state, or national government might be next

Local programs such as these are likely to spur additional green roof construction, validate at least some benefits, and make green roofs more attractive options for compliance or investment. They might also help to settle outstanding issues associated with green roofs and other low-impact design solutions, including how

Green roofs are gaining a foothold in Washington, D.C., where many federal agencies are using them on their properties to control stormwater, save energy, and prolong the roof's life.

agencies can track their locations; how to inform new owners about the function, maintenance, and legal responsibilities associated with them; how the local government can get access to and inspect them; and how authorities should deal with owners who won't maintain the controls on their property (Slone and Evans 2003). For now, green roofs and related measures lack the engineering attributes associated with traditional stormwater controls such as detention ponds. Many officials are struggling to resolve their position of being caught between an old system that does not work, a new approach that requires taxpayer-financed incentives to get widespread adoption, and the obligation to comply with the Clean Water Act.

Section 438 of the 2007 Energy Independence and Security Act might also help bring some clarity. It requires large new U. S. federal government building projects to either use practices that infiltrate, evapotranspirate, harvest, and/or reuse rainfall to prevent any off-site discharge from most storms or to design, build, and maintain the project so as to maintain the predevelopment rate, volume, duration, and temperature for stormwater runoff (EPA 2009b). As one of the world's largest landholders commits to using green infrastructure and demonstrates its efficacy, more state and local governments might find it easier to integrate green roofs and other low-impact stormwater controls into their own laws and regulations. The experience of pioneering cities such as those described above might smooth the process for those who follow.

For designers, developers, and owners, following the minutiae of the policymaking process is not necessarily important. But being aware that the process is happening is important. Regulations are continuously changing, sometimes dramatically. Keeping abreast of new and potential incentives and requirements will help streamline approvals and possibly save the owner money.

This green roof, at the Gary Comer Youth Center in Chicago, was designed to support perennials, tall grasses, and vegetables.

4 Designing and Building Your Green Roof

Key Points

- Advice for owners:

  Clarify your objectives so you can decide whether a green roof is right for you.

  Choose designers with green roof experience. Landscapes at grade and conventional roofs are not the same.

  Know that your construction documents might be your only recourse if problems arise. Detailed is better.

  Have a knowledgeable representative or project manager on site during installation.

  Invest in maintenance. Don't spend your whole budget on design.

- Advice for designers:

  Listen to your client's objectives, and make sure a green roof is right for the project.

  Know what you don't know and where to find people who do.

  Don't run on autopilot. Specify only the components necessary to achieve the project's objectives.

  Default to what has been proven to work. Don't use the project for experimentation unless your client explicitly agrees.

  Remain engaged. When things go wrong, learn from and fix mistakes.

The design process

The green roof design process, like a green roof itself, is a hybrid. Most landscape projects do not take place on a building or as part of the construction of the building itself, and most building projects do not involve living elements. Thoughtful and appropriate design choices are always important, but on a green roof project the impact of these choices can show up in unexpected places. The cost of careful design is almost always lower than the cost of failure. Interdisciplinary cooperation is especially important to ensure that all of the elements of the project, from the structural to the horticultural, complement and reinforce each other.

Establishing objectives: educate yourself up front

Owners or developers considering a green roof should learn what living with one entails. Try to find projects similar to your own with green roofs and see how they are working after installation. Do they look good? Have there been leaks or other problems? Are the plants well established? Would those owners choose a green roof again? If you are sure that a green roof is right for your project, the more clearly you articulate your objectives for that roof to your design team at the earliest stages of the process, the more likely it is that the design will satisfy those objectives.

Similarly, it is important for the designer to clarify the client's objectives before the design process begins in earnest. "Don't put pencil to paper unless you know why you want a green roof," says green roof engineer and designer Charlie Miller. Some building owners might be focused on performance, others might want to incorporate as many green features into the building as possible on altruistic, marketing, or other grounds. If a client proposes a green roof, it's incumbent on the designer to understand what, exactly, the client wants to achieve and to make sure the owner understands what a green roof is (not necessarily a roof garden), what it will look like (especially early in its life), what level of effort is needed to sustain the roof (this will depend on the design), and how much it is going to cost, both up front and over its lifetime.

This kind of inquiry, of course, is an important part of the design process for any landscape or construction project and any significant aspect of a large building project. But the green roof is a new design concept to most people. This might make it a more desirable option in some cases and more intimidating in others. Some people will be familiar with green roofs only through articles and images that highlight spectacular but unique projects that have little relevance to a standard commercial or residential job. In other cases, a client might have objectives that a green roof can effectively satisfy, but the client might be unaware of this potential.

Determine whether green roof is a good way to help achieve those objectives

Even if a green roof appears to be a good potential design solution, it might not be the best choice in the context of the project. It might be difficult to keep plants alive, for example, on a roof that is shaded by other buildings for most of the day. A low-rise building surrounded by plants, such as maple trees, that produce and disperse a lot of viable seed, might make maintenance too onerous for a green roof to be practical. On a suburban site with a lot of available land, measures such as rain gardens and porous paving might be easier to implement and a more cost-effective way to manage stormwater.

Even when a green roof is theoretically feasible on a project, if you leave aesthetics aside and compare it to other sustainable building or ecosystem service tools by discrete function, a green roof might seem like an unacceptably expensive solution. A white roof can save energy and usually costs less to install. Rain gardens and bioretention swales in paved areas can capture stormwater runoff and can be designed and installed without directly implicating the building, making the process much easier and less expensive.

But here, too, the context and details of the project matter. In a densely built city, with less land available for at-grade measures such as rain gardens, a green roof might be one of the few viable green options for a new project or retrofit. An owner focused on long-term costs and performance might choose a more expensive but durable green roof over a shorter-lived white roof.

In addition, green roofs provide an aggregation of benefits that can make their higher initial costs worthwhile. A green roof designed primarily to satisfy stormwater code requirements might also serve as an accessible or visual amenity space or help to lower energy costs on a low-slung industrial building. Public benefits, such as a single building's modest contribution to mitigating the urban heat island effect and reducing stormwater run-off into local rivers and streams or providing a patch of urban green and a pleasant view for workers and residents in neighboring buildings might be impossible to quantify but important to the client. The visible evidence of the owner's commitment to sustainability might enhance the building's value or the owner's reputation in the community.

Deploy a full spectrum of knowledge and skills

While green roof design and construction require a range of disciplines, there is no template or checklist of necessary professionals for a green roof design team. No one person will hold all of the necessary expertise, and each member of the team should be fully aware of his or her own specific responsibilities and those

Good roofing details are an important part of green roof design and installation. The flashings on this vent were done well, the drains are well clear of planted areas, and rainwater and any condensation will drain quickly away from the area through the large-graded stone.

held by others. Most important is that everyone, especially the lead designer, should be cognizant of gaps in knowledge and how to fill them in a manner that strengthens the design.

The team should include people who are experienced and well versed in green roof materials, components, standards and testing methods, and design paradigms as well as sound roof construction and horticulture. An architect, for example, might be able to design a structurally sound roof, but might not appreciate materials compatibility and drainage issues introduced by the overburden of a green roof. That's not a problem as long as the architect recognizes the need to consult others who do understand those issues.

Similarly, the green roof team must ensure that the non-green aspects of the roof, such as waterproofing and flashings, are integrated successfully with the green aspects and are not undermined during installation of the overburden. Roof leaks most often occur where horizontal and vertical sections meet, such as parapet walls and penetrations, so flashings and other details must be carefully and appropriately designed (NRCA 2009).

The leader of the design team need not engage separate individuals or firms for each subset of required knowledge, but the team should, across its membership, have access to all of the information necessary to produce a good result. On a design/build project, the team should also have a reliable network of suppliers to ensure that materials are consistent and of high quality. If the project is being put out for bid, the designers should know enough about the components of a green roof assembly that they can write specifications.

The design solution and the product solution

Because green roofs are new to most designers and installers, selecting an experienced firm or team of firms to design and build your green roof will make it more likely a project will satisfy your objectives. For a designer, researching components and choosing those most likely to satisfy your client's objectives and cultivating relationships with an experienced installation team if you operate under a design/build model are most likely to result in a successful project. Sometimes, however, a more standardized approach makes sense.

A custom approach (the design solution) need not be prohibitively expensive. Specialized firms comprising people with a lot of experience designing, installing, and maintaining green roof systems can help firm up objectives for the project and specify a system using only the components needed to achieve those objectives. Modifications that save money without compromising the roof's function might be possible. A custom-designed system will be tailored to the site and the owner's budget constraints.

Providers of the design solution might be multidisciplinary firms, architects or landscape architects, specialty divisions of roofing companies, or installers or consultants who specialize exclusively in green roofs. If the project is being put out for competitive bidding, a strong design that is well thought out early in the process will result in more realistic bids and fewer problems during construction. If a design/build approach is taken, the inclusion of experienced green roof designers throughout the process is likely to result in better communication about the importance of different components and characteristics and often a shorter, more efficient, and less costly installation process. A design/build approach also gives the owner a single-source point of contact and responsibility in the case of any problems. On a design/bid/build project, responsibility might be more diffuse and more difficult to pin down. This should be addressed in the construction documents with specific and detailed allocations of responsibility.

In the current green roof marketplace, "experienced" can be a relative term. Don't assume that a high-profile design firm is necessarily your best choice, especially if the firm has completed few green roof projects. Undertake due diligence before hiring a design firm. Having one or two green roofs on its project list does not always mean a firm has the wherewithal to do the best job for you. Gorgeous professional photographs taken shortly after installation do not reveal how the roof has stood the test of time. Visit installations if possible, especially older ones, to see how they are performing and how any postinstallation problems were handled. Talk to clients and, if possible, to the building's operations and maintenance team, if the roof falls under their care.

A product solution can be a standardized above-the-membrane green roof assembly or series of components such as prevegetated modular trays. These systems are easy for the designer to specify, and some have worked very well in the field. If there is a problem after installation, the owner has a single source to call. Sometimes a product solution is the only way to green a roof (see "Prevegetated installation options" in chapter 2).

It can be difficult, however, to adjust a comprehensive proprietary solution to the particular requirements or objectives of your project. The team involved with a product solution will not necessarily include a plant expert who can choose the best plants and growing medium for the project. If specifications are not tightly written to discourage inappropriate substitutions, products can be swapped out during the installation process without consideration of differences in performance. And the performance of high-quality products depends on skilled installation, something that manufacturers are not always well placed to provide.

You might also be buying components you do not need if they are only available as part of a package. In addition to the extra cost this entails and the higher labor costs associated with the installation of a more complex system, the extra components can in some cases do more harm than good, potentially diminishing the system's functional capability, says landscape architect Jeffrey Bruce.

Regardless of the approach used, it is important that someone on the design team have horticultural knowledge specific to a rooftop environment. A designer specifying a green roof system in addition to other aspects of a large project should hire a horticulturist who specializes in planted roof systems, says construction specifier Ken Hercenberg. Selecting appropriate medium and plants and determining an appropriate maintenance regime should be done by an expert.

On any project, owners should be on guard against aggressive product sales pitches or designs that are insufficiently attentive to the project's objectives, situations that can arise with either a design or a product solution. An inappropriate design—

for example, one featuring plants inaccurately described to the client as low maintenance—is as bad as an unsuitable or unnecessary product.

Be mindful of the basics

Some basic criteria apply to every project. The building must support the weight of the green roof with mature plants when fully saturated. The design must provide adequate drainage and preserve the integrity of the waterproofing membrane, especially at vulnerable points at edges and penetrations. The plant palette selected should reflect the microclimates on the roof, including shaded and protected areas and those with more exposure, as well as the regional climate and its rainfall, aridity, frost and heat zones, and wind intensity. Materials with a proven track record of performance and a long life span should be specified (Miller 2009b).

On a deeper level, the design details should be geared toward the desired performance, whether that means stormwater retention, great looks, or something else. Various design paradigms are discussed later in this chapter, but there are a few general points worth keeping in mind. For example, a green roof is usually included in a project to provide one or more environmental benefits, so it's often safe to assume that the owner and the designer want to maximize the amount of ecological output while minimizing inputs, including materials and labor, as much as possible. In many cases, the simplest possible design will be best, whichever paradigm applies.

The design team and building owner should also consider the trade-offs involved in various design choices. If, for example, the desired plant palette requires irrigation, that will not only mean higher design and installation costs, it will also have long-term implications: The system will have to be checked and perhaps adjusted seasonally, adding to the maintenance ledger. Irrigation can also make a roof more hospitable to weeds, another maintenance consideration. Water is a limited resource in some areas, and the plastic from which most irrigation systems are made adds to the ecological footprint of the project. Some aspects of the LEED certification program discourage irrigation after establishment. This is not to say that permanent irrigation should never be designed into a project, only that it should be a conscious choice and the client should be aware of all of the implications of design choices. For more on green roof irrigation, see "Special design considerations and challenges" later in this chapter.

Similarly, a design using unproven components or plants not commonly grown on a green roof should only be undertaken when the client is fully apprised of its experimental nature. An untested component that an inventor, a website, or a salesperson raves about might well be too good to be true. Even plants that are drought-tolerant or that thrive with little intervention at grade might not be appropriate choices for a roof environment. Intuition is not enough to justify the use of unproven materials or plants unless the nature of the project is explicitly experimental.

Finally, the design details should account for all of the activity required to maintain the green roof over the long term. Even on roofs not conceived as amenity spaces, access must be provided for maintenance. Even on roofs without irrigation systems, water will probably be needed during establishment or long droughts. Maintenance tasks might require a power source. On a roof planted with species that produce a lot of dry and dormant biomass, such as taller grasses, maintenance is easier if the crew

This frost-free hydrant can supply water for supplemental irrigation any time it's needed, all year round.

can remove the materials without having to worry about getting a visitor elevator dirty.

Consider long-term costs in the design phase

Economics are among the most important implications of any design choice. The additional cost of a green roof might be partially offset by incentives or by the longer life span predicted for green roofs based on the protection they offer the membrane. But even simple extensive versions, without elaborate designs or plant palettes, are still more expensive than a conventional roof. Some of this extra cost is associated with the more complex assembly, but it can seem excessive in some cases.

It is therefore important during the design process to remember that maintenance, especially during establishment, is key to green roof success and has its own cost. The owner should allocate a reasonable amount of the project's budget toward this function. The simpler the design and the more proven the plant palette, the less onerous maintenance costs—both money and labor—will be. Green roofs can be designed to be relatively low maintenance, especially after the establishment period, but with rare exceptions ignoring maintenance or giving it short shrift is inviting problems.

Write strong specifications

Specifications are the written technical details of the materials and procedures associated with a construction project. They establish the performance standards for the design and determine what, if any, changes can be made to those materials and procedures during construction (Harris 1988). Construction specifications are either performance based or prescriptive, the latter requiring the use of certain products, manufacturers, vendors, or contractors for each aspect of a project. Specifications for green roof projects should include:

- a summary of the project, including the scope of work and reference to related sections;
- definitions and references to standards such as FLL guidelines and ASTM standards;
- performance requirements;
- submittals, including product data, shop drawings, and samples;
- procedures for delivery, storage, and handling of materials on site;
- procedures for quality assurance, including field supervision, product data, test results, limitations on substitutions, and certification from the manufacturer that the waterproofing membrane is compatible with a green roof system;
- procedures for installation, including site preparation, inspections, surface preparation, safety measures, membrane protection, and planting;
- maintenance requirements.

Proper specification of a green roof requires understanding the contribution of each component and how different parts of the system work together. A green roof design should not be overspecified with unnecessary components, which can happen when specifiers select proprietary systems as a shortcut, or underspecified so that performance objectives cannot be met, which can happen when, for example, a designer neglects to address the hydraulic implications of a steep slope. Designers should not copy and paste unfamiliar specifications. Although careful specification requires time and attention that can be scarce on a large project, poorly written specifications can undermine a green roof's performance or even result in a failed project. They can also generate unrealistic bids from contractors.

Specifications should be detailed and clear so that the appropriate components are sourced and used, inappropriate substitutions are prevented, performance is optimized, and responsibility for maintenance and any needed repairs is assigned. While such an approach might seem unreasonably burdensome to busy professionals and tradespeople engaged with many aspects of a project beyond the green roof, it's in the owner's interest to insist upon such an approach because the construction documents are part of the legal record of the project and the only avenue for recourse if something goes wrong.

Specifications that do not include assigned performance values risk undermining the project's design intent while leaving the owner with no means of satisfaction. "If no performance values are assigned and there's a failure, but all their contract says is 'provide soil,' you have no recourse," says landscape architect Jeffrey Bruce. "Or 'soil that supports plant life.' What does that mean? Algae is a form of plant life, would that meet the intent of the specification? Defining performance is important. That should be in the contract, or part of the submittal process."

This sample specification (courtesy of Roofscapes) illustrates one way to address performance requirements:

Vegetated roof covering system shall:
1. Support a perennial vegetated ground cover.
2. Provide efficient drainage of moisture that is in excess of that required for the vigorous growth of the installed vegetation.
3. Protect roof waterproofing materials from damage caused by exposure to ultraviolet radiation, physical abuse, and rapid temperature fluctuations.
4. Retain 1.00 inches (2.5 cm) of moisture at maximum water capacity, in accordance with the referenced ASTM E-2397 standard.
5. The wet dead weight of this system shall not exceed 20 pounds per square foot (97.6 kg per square meter), in accordance with the referenced ASTM E-2397 standard.
6. Continue to perform as designed for the duration of the warranty period, without a requirement to amend or refresh the media.

A complete sample specification for a typical green roof project is provided at the back of the book.

Good specifications, including details about executing the design on site such as inspections and surface preparations, are also in the interest of the team installing the project. Construction crews might be unfamiliar with green roof components, so instructions for installing fabrics and drainage sheets should be very specific to ensure overlaps are appropriate and materials are installed right-side up. The specifications should also spell out when installation ends, when maintenance begins, and when establishment ends, because these terms are not well defined within the industry.

The reality in the field, however, is that most green roof specifications, especially on large and complicated new construction projects, are not particularly detailed. Options for responsibly delegating decisions on materials including growing medium and plants are not always exercised. A common approach, says Ken Hercenberg, is for the lead designer to make the green roof design details the responsibility of the general contractor and specify a roofing company and a plant supplier who will work together to provide single-source accountability. But this kind of delegation should reflect confidence built on relationships forged during successful projects—not on mere unwillingness to grapple with technical details. "We may not be soil engineers, but we align ourselves with reputable firms who can give us advice," says roofing company executive Jim Stamer.

It is also important to make sure that construction documents are properly cross-referenced and that the project team knows where all of the details of the green roof design can be found. Under the widely used MasterFormat system established by the Construction Specifications Institute, roofing falls under Division 7 (thermal and moisture protection), whereas most landscape details fall under Division 32 (exterior improvements). A planting plan or maintenance specification for a green roof, for example, might appear under Division 32 and be overlooked or forgotten while the project team is focused on Division 7. Subcontractors accustomed to landscape projects at grade might not notice materials such as fabrics or drainage boards specified under Division 7.

The installation process

Because green roofs are not yet well understood in the design and construction industries, having the whole project team engaged throughout the design and installation process is ideal but not always achievable. Especially when a project is put out to bid after the design phase, the importance of decisions and the process that led to choices of one material or approach rather than the available alternatives can get lost, with unfortunate or disastrous results for the project.

It's impossible to anticipate or account for every hypothetical problem that might arise during the construction phase. Sometimes events beyond anyone's control—a highway closure that prevents the timely delivery of live plants, or a mistake by the shipping company that sends auto parts rather than plants to the building site—can sabotage a project. But a lot of problems can be prevented by thoughtful planning, good communication, and attention to detail. Owners should consider taking extra precautions to ensure that the installation is done as effectively and efficiently as possible, with all of the important elements of the design intact.

Preserve the integrity of the design through the installation process

Even the best design, if not properly installed, can deliver subpar performance or fail outright. Attention to detail and quality control are just as important during the installation phase and will help ensure that the design intent is realized in the completed project.

Resist inappropriate value engineering

The process of value engineering has become associated with cost cutting for its own sake, even though as originally conceived it stood in opposition to reductions in quality or function (Johnson 2007). In today's economic climate, the desire to avoid unnecessary spending is understandable. But when new technologies, such as green roofs, are not well understood by everyone on the project team, the implications of changes to specifications might not be appreciated. For example, a contractor unfamiliar with the properties of green roof medium might believe that using soil dug up from the building site during construction is a good way to save money. Or a contractor more familiar with landscapes at grade might change a plant list without a full understanding of

ing most of the plants cut off from sunlight and air circulation. This will require either a lot of space for spreading out the trays or a tight schedule whereby the trays arrive on site just before they are to be installed.

Have a knowledgeable representative on site

Even the strongest and most detailed design and specifications can be undermined in the absence of quality control on site during construction. It is in the owner's interest to have someone—an owner's representative, a project manager, or a construction administrator—on site throughout the process. While this is an added expense, failure is also expensive, especially on a large project.

A green roof failure might not be obvious right away, because plants might never properly establish or die out slowly if planted in poor medium or if drainage components are improperly installed. By the time the magnitude of the problem is apparent, the green roof might have to be disassembled to identify the cause. Even when the cause is established, the project team will have moved on, and sorting out responsibility might be difficult or impossible. An experienced representative can prevent this kind of disaster.

Whatever his or her title, the person fulfilling this role should understand how a green roof assembly works and be deeply familiar with the project specifications. The representative or manager need not be an expert in every aspect of the design, but he or she must be able to assess potential problems, make decisions, and know whom to seek out for technical advice or to confirm that components meet specified standards.

Provide for long-term performance and success

For many clients, one of the key selling points of a green roof is its longevity. In places such as Germany where green roofs are plentiful, they have been shown to extend the life span of a roof's waterproofing membrane substantially (Porsche and Köhler 2003). Designers should therefore be mindful of a green roof's long potential life when selecting plants and materials, thinking in terms of decades rather than a couple of seasons. Most clients won't want to regularly replace large numbers of plants or remove parts of the assembly to replace less durable components.

To maximize this benefit, as well as stormwater management performance and more subjective qualities such as an attractive appearance, the green roof has to reach a state of equilibrium wherein the system can sustain itself with little intervention. This usually takes about two years for an extensive roof planted with hardy succulents; other plant palettes might take longer. Some designs, such as geometric planting layouts or those using plants that spread or self-seed aggressively, will require a high level of maintenance in perpetuity to retain a consistent appearance. For more information about the level of effort required to maintain different green roof designs, see the design paradigms discussed later in this chapter.

The establishment phase: maintenance is crucial

As in most landscape projects, plants are best installed on a green roof in a juvenile state, during which it's easiest for them to adapt to their new environment. It usually takes a year or two for most green roof plants to grow to maturity and cover most of the vegetated roof area. Most of the maintenance on an extensive green roof is done during this establishment phase, at the end of which the system should be reasonably self-sustaining. Management of the roof during this period can ensure, or undermine, its long-term success.

Maintenance visits during establishment usually focus on weeding and keeping an eye on the newly installed plants' health. The timing of maintenance visits early in a green roof's life is especially important. If the roof is planted in the autumn, there will be little immediate weed pressure if the growing medium is reasonably weed-free. If planting is done in the spring, however, frequent short visits in the first weeks after plants are installed and visits throughout the growing season timed to prevent the seeding of common and pernicious green roof weeds will help to keep new weeds under control. Understanding the lifecycles of common green roof weeds is important for effective maintenance.

Just-installed plugs are vulnerable to damage before their roots start to develop in their new environment. The exposed medium is subject to weed pressure.

Three months after installation, the plants have acclimated to their new environment and begun to grow and spread.

Specify maintenance in detail

Some installers include one or two years of maintenance as a standard part of their contract. In other cases the owner takes responsibility for the roof right away and presumably assigns maintenance to in-house staff or a subcontractor. It is crucial that, however it is allocated, responsibility for maintenance is clearly defined in the project specifications.

If the installer will be maintaining the roof during establishment, the details of the program should also be defined precisely. For example, if there is a patio area, is cleaning of the pavers and weeding in between the pavers—a time-consuming task—included in required maintenance? Or should weeding be focused on the expanse of vegetated area? These issues should be spelled out in the specifications.

It is also useful to set goals for the end of the establishment period that are as specific as possible, for example, 80 or 90 percent plant coverage after two years. It can be difficult, however, to pin such definitions down. What if most of the roof has virtually complete plant coverage, but one spot is extremely sparse? What does "weed-free" mean in a dynamic environment? Well-designed specifications, good communication, a maintenance team experienced with green roofs, and the flexibility to see each project as a unique and constantly changing landscape will help to address many problems at a stage when they can be solved relatively easily.

If the owner chooses to take responsibility for the green roof immediately or before plants are fully established, the designer or installer should give the facilities staff or subcontractor all of the information necessary to care for the roof during the establishment phase and over the long term. The handover materials should include, at a minimum, a plant list; suggested schedules for watering, weeding, and fertilizing; and instructions for keeping drains and other systems, such as irrigation lines if there are any, functioning properly.

Stay engaged over the long term

Even after it reaches a relatively steady state, a green roof, like any landscape, is a dynamic system and will change from season to season and year to year. Although it is natural, after one project is installed, for designers to move on to the next project, all landscape projects reward sustained attention. Which plants easily adapt to this kind of site? Which ones struggle? Do the non-living materials perform as advertised? Observations like these, and making and tracking changes as appropriate in response, do not only help keep a green roof in good working order. They also inform and strengthen subsequent designs in countless ways.

This is especially true of extensive green roofs, because they are such a new technology, at least in North America, and because they are intended to last such a long time. There have been and will continue to be problems as designers and installers determine over time and in some cases by trial and error what works best in different climates and microclimates. The lack of an established North American green roof industry has significant downsides. But there is also an upside in that the marketplace is ripe for innovation.

In Europe, green roofs are standardized utilitarian products. While there is a need here for this kind of inexpensive, no-nonsense green roof, there is also potential to do more—to optimize stormwater performance, to enhance energy benefits, to identify a wider range of plants that will survive on a roof while providing benefits for threatened pollinators or other wildlife, and to otherwise design for better performance.

Academic research will contribute to these potential improvements, but important data could also come from designers and owners who take a long-term interest in what happens on their roofs, use their experience to inform later projects, and share information. Which plants go dormant during long, hot summers? Which ones establish quickly to provide cover but later give way to more dominant species? Does the growing medium hold its physical properties, or does it lose volume or porosity in a few years? Does an irrigation system, even if used only in extreme conditions, contribute to a system's longevity? The best green roof designers and installers know they have a responsibility for a project's success, even when their contractual obligations have technically been discharged. Most of them prefer to maintain their own projects whenever possible. They learn from mistakes as well as successes, and they are not afraid to challenge their assumptions. These are the people who will move the industry forward. If you are a designer, you should emulate them. If you are looking for a designer, you should hire people like this.

Green roof design paradigms: simple extensive green roofs

Perhaps the greatest potential for large-scale green roof construction lies with the most basic design paradigm: an extensive roof with a minimal depth of medium supporting a limited palette of tough plants designed to be as self-sustaining as possible over time.

This large, simple, extensive green roof in Germany is about fifteen years old. Green roofs of this type are commonly installed to control stormwater and perform other functions.

Simple extensive green roofs have several common characteristics: mixed hardy succulent plants in random patterns and in most cases a relatively simple assembly including plants, growing medium, drainage, and a root barrier if needed. Their advantages

include relatively low cost (in some markets, $10 or less per square foot), relatively light weight, relatively low maintenance after establishment, and good stormwater performance in most climates with about 3 to 4 inches (7.5 to 10 cm) of medium. However, simple extensive green roofs also have some disadvantages, including a limited plant palette, which means lower biodiversity, and limited design options. In addition, the stormwater performance of very thin roofs might be diminished.

This kind of green roof might be included in a project to satisfy stormwater codes; to reduce reliance on other stormwater management options that might not be feasible, cost-effective, or desirable on a particular site; to help obtain LEED certification; or to take advantage of incentives for green roof construction. It's a realistic option for retrofitting many existing buildings, and it represents a sweet spot of sorts, providing a good level of ecological benefit for a relatively modest cost.

In some situations a basic green roof will be at best purely functional and at worst an undesired element of the project, included with reluctance to comply with code requirements or other mandates. But a purely functional green roof can cost about the same amount or even save money on some projects. In a densely built city, for example, a green roof can provide an alternative to traditional stormwater infrastructure measures such as a below-ground concrete vault. "Those have to support and retain a lot of water, they're heavy, they require a lot of structure and waterproofing," says roofing company executive Jim Stamer. "You might be able to spend a similar amount on a green roof and retain the same amount of stormwater." In addition, says Stamer, a green roof, even one not designed for regular use and visitation, can be a valued and marketable asset for a building owner.

That was the case for a Hilton Hotel in Baltimore. This was a new building on an approximately 5-acre (2-ha) site adjacent to the city's convention center. While the site had been impervious, the city wanted to bring the pervious area up to 20 percent on the lot for better stormwater management. The original design achieved this by building in a large sand filter under Eutaw Street in addition to a small planted area at grade.

The green roof on Baltimore's Hilton Hotel helps to manage stormwater and gives the facility, which is adjacent to the city's convention center, a marketing advantage. Photograph courtesy of Furbish Company

During design development, however, the project team discovered there was not enough physical space under the roadway to build the design in a cost-effective manner, and the team settled on a 32,000 square foot (2973 square meter) green roof for stormwater control. Installing the green roof as a built-in-place, rather than modular, assembly brought the cost in at less than that originally planned for the sand filter. Installer Michael Furbish says that Hilton was pleased with the result because it made economic sense, it reinforced Hilton's reputation as a sustainable company, it provided a more attractive view for patrons in rooms looking out over the roof toward the downtown baseball stadium, and it would satisfy the desire on the part of many conference organizers to use facilities with green features. The client's clarity of intention helped the design team determine the right solution.

Although it is not accessible, except for maintenance visits, the roof is visible from many of the hotel's guest rooms.

Guests with a view of the Camden Yards baseball stadium can now gaze out over a green roof. Photograph courtesy of Furbish Company

Make the best of limited design options

The most significant downside to an extensive roof is the lack of design options. Most basic extensive green roofs look about the same. While some people appreciate the neat and tidy carpetlike appearance of an extensive green roof, especially when it is well maintained and mostly free of weeds, others find any roof planted exclusively with hardy succulents to be visually dull. Its appearance can be improved by using a greater variety of hardy succulent species, which will add texture and color. Planting in strict patterns can be done on a thin-profile green roof, if plants are installed as plugs rather than cuttings, but the higher cost and effort involved and increased maintenance required puts such an approach in another category.

Green roofs are a feature on several dormitories at Swarthmore College in southeastern Pennsylvania. The roofs installed in 2008 on the upper sections of David Kemp Hall are less visible and accessible than some of the lower green roofs on campus. To save money on installation and simplify maintenance, these sections were planted exclusively with a mix of sedum cuttings. But the fifteen different species used makes this roof especially attractive.

These green roofs on David Kemp Hall at Swarthmore College were planted with a mix of sedum cuttings that established quickly and provided a lot of color and texture for a low price. This photo was taken one year after planting.

Leave little room for error

Another potential difficulty with a very basic green roof is that in an austere system, any deficiencies in the design, specifications, or components will have a greater impact. While an extensive green roof has a relatively simple design and appearance, each component has to perform all necessary functions or the system can fail. Here, again, an experienced and knowledgeable project team will be most likely to deliver quality and value, accurately assess site conditions, and design the project to work within those conditions.

Green roof designer Angie Duhrman had worked on a lot of projects when she was hired to design her first in the hot and humid Deep South. It would also be the first green roof in Birmingham, Alabama. To stay within budget and to make LEED certification easier by requiring fewer inputs, the team decided on an extensive system with a maximum medium depth of 4 inches (10 cm). Loading capacity on the large roof—more than 83,000 square feet (7719 square meters) are vegetated—was also a consideration.

Duhrman has an academic background in horticulture but consulted with a regional grower to make the best selection among the hardy succulents suited to the conditions on site, because summer temperatures in Birmingham frequently surpass 90°F (32°C) and rainfall varies considerably. The grower had installed his own green roof a few years before and knew which species would work best. Twelve species of *Sedum* and *Delosperma* were custom propagated.

Although construction of the building and installation of the membrane were completed in April 2007, Duhrman convinced the owner and general contractor to wait until late September to install the rest of the assembly and the plugs to promote better establishment under less stressful conditions. The next year, however, was extremely dry. The roof has no permanent irrigation system but was watered during this period to keep the plants alive. The plants have established well, according to Jim Burton, who oversees quarterly maintenance visits under the five-year contract. Cuttings are taken and spread during spring and autumn to fill in any remaining bare spots.

Page 158, top: This green roof in Birmingham, Alabama, was the designer's first project in such a hot, humid climate. Photograph courtesy of Tecta

Page 158, bottom: Other aspects of the project were completed in the spring, but the installation of the green roof assembly was de-layed until the autumn to make it easier for the plants to establish. Photograph courtesy of Tecta

Left: The plants, twelve species of *Sedum* and *Delosperma*, were selected in consultation with a regional grower and custom prop-agated for the project. Photograph courtesy of Tecta

The experienced team, specialty supplier, and regular maintenance associated with this project did not unduly raise costs. Duhrman recalls the overburden, including the maintenance contract, as costing about $11 to $12 per square foot.

Pushing the basic design envelope

Even within this practical design paradigm choices will sometimes have to be made. You can get a permit, good stormwater performance, and the cheapest or lightest possible green roof. You might not, however, be able to get all of these at once. Though it is not a zero-sum game, pushing the envelope on one aspect of a basic roof's design is likely to have an impact on other aspects.

Designing for light weight

Especially in the case of retrofits, weight can be the issue that makes or breaks a roof greening opportunity. Sometimes this problem can be solved by design. One way to lighten the load of the assembly is to make the profile as thin as possible by using less growing medium and limiting, to the extent feasible, the materials and layers used. The price of this approach can be severe limitations on the plant palette and a diminution of storm-water performance. But a very thin green roof can survive and even thrive if carefully planned and approached with realistic expectations.

When Falls Church, Virginia, environmentalist Jeanette Stewart was working to make her condominium community more environmentally sensitive, a green roof was an obvious choice. Several obstacles stood in her way, however, including structural limitations and a lack of resources for long-term maintenance. By shopping around for the thinnest and lightest system and using a plant palette limited to a few very tough *Sedum* species, Stewart was able to get a green roof that met her stringent requirements and needs.

Loading capacity is often an issue with retrofit projects. This building, part of a 1960s-era condominium complex, could only accommodate 15 pounds per square foot (73.2 kg per square meter), so the owner had to shop around to find the lightest possible green roof system. Photograph by Jeanette Stewart

The 1960s-era buildings of the community, Yorktowne Square, have a maximum weight capacity of only 15 pounds per square foot (73.2 kg per square meter), which is less than some of the simplest green roof assemblies. The first assembly Stewart considered pushed that envelope, and neither Stewart nor that manufacturer were comfortable going forward. Additional research led her to an assembly by Virginia Beach–based Building Logics that weighed 13.5 pounds per square foot (65.9 kg per

Few plants can survive in only 2 inches (5 cm) of growing medium, so a simple plant palette of three tough sedums was chosen. Photograph by Jeanette Stewart

One advantage of such an austere system is that most weeds cannot survive. Tree seedlings blown in from the surrounding landscape spring up but die soon afterward, lacking enough water and nutrients. Photograph by Linda McIntyre

square meter) when fully vegetated and saturated. That low weight was achieved in part by a waterproofing membrane that did not require a separate root barrier and a drainage system designed to quickly discharge water from stronger storms. Also key to the lightness of the system was the minimal amount of growing medium—only 2 inches (5 cm).

Not many plants can survive in such a harsh environment. Only three tough species, *Sedum album*, *S. sexangulare*, and *S. reflexum*, were used. The plants were never irrigated, but they established well enough to survive a hurricane shortly after installation in 2003. After establishment, they maintained good cover even during the region's usually hot and often dry summers. Access to the roof is difficult; after some weeding during its first full growing season, no additional maintenance has been done, but the austere conditions help to keep weed pressure down.

A green roof this thin is not ideal for managing stormwater. But Stewart installed 950-gallon (3610-L) cisterns to collect runoff from both the green roof and a conventional roof on another building in the community, and the results have been impressive given the limitations on the design. A graduate student monitoring runoff found during one month in the summer of 2007, for example, an 85 percent reduction of runoff from small storms with less than 0.5 inch (1.25 cm) of rainfall.

To reduce weight, horticulturist and modular green roof system designer David MacKenzie usually works with the depth of the medium in his company's green roof modules. Their system, filled with 4 inches (10 cm) of medium, weighs about 30 pounds per square foot (146.4 kg per square meter) when saturated. To reduce the weight, he might add a course of lightweight fill and reduce the depth of medium to as shallow as 2.5 inches (6.25 cm).

That's what MacKenzie did with the roof on a western Michigan transit hub. A previous green roof application had failed, but owing to structural constraints there was little leeway to provide a richer horticultural environment.

Sometimes, says MacKenzie, such changes will affect the plant palette. He would not, for example, use taller sedums (such as *Sedum* 'Autumn Joy') in 2.5 inches (6.25 cm) of soil. Instead he

An earlier green roof application on this transit hub in Michigan dried out and died, but the building's structural capacity did not allow for a deep course of growing medium.

Modules were assembled with a course of lightweight fill and less than 3 inches (7.5 cm) of growing medium. Plants were carefully selected for their ability to survive in such a system.

might use alliums for similar height and color effects. In addition, a narrow substrate depth might make an irrigation system an appealing or even necessary option. MacKenzie says such a system would probably be used regularly during hot summer months in many parts of the United States.

Designing for low cost

Green roof consultant Peter Philippi, who worked in Germany before establishing a business in the United States, says that as green roof components and systems become more standardized, consistent, and reliable, the market will become more efficient and prices will drop. He predicts that competition among suppliers and installers and adoption of improved conveyance methods, such as the more sophisticated pneumatic blower trucks used in Germany and Switzerland, will also make green roofs more affordable in North America (Philippi 2006).

But as the Birmingham, Alabama, project discussed above shows, good design can also reduce rather than raise costs. Experienced designers can assess ways to save money without compromising a roof's function, longevity, or safety. Landscape architect Jason King was able to safely eliminate most of the metal edging on a project and save about $2.50 per square foot. He also tries hard to find appropriate local materials to save on transport costs, as well as for the ecological benefits.

No single tweak will necessarily save a lot of money, King says, but factoring costs into decision-making throughout the process can cut the price per square foot almost in half on some projects. "That can make the difference between a green roof be-

In Europe, the cost of green roof components such as growing medium have come down as the market has become more competitive. Many expect that will happen in North America as well.

ing built or having it value engineered out of the project." Similarly, says designer and installer Chris Goode, by coming on board early in the project, his company can save money by specifying a membrane that does not need a separate root barrier and otherwise keeping unnecessary components out of the design. His company has been able to install extensive roofs in New York City for as little as $10 per square foot. Measures like these, of course, should only be taken by designers who fully understand the impact of the proposed changes on the system as a whole.

Designer and installer Greg Raymond makes a related point: If fewer people can bring a full range of expertise to design and build a project, it will cost less. Projects that begin with a reasonable estimate can find that markups by all of the contractors double the price. Raymond, whose firm maintains green roofs installed by others as well as their own projects, also says this line of business has had an impact on the design side. Simplifying maintenance, he says, translates into a lower-cost green roof for the owner. Maintaining projects also gives a designer a better idea of which plants and designs hold up well over time.

A growing array of incentives and grant opportunities is also available to help make green roofs a more economical choice. Options should be thoroughly researched early in the design process. Whereas most green building incentives are provided at

Specialized equipment makes the transport and installation of components easy, fast, and less expensive. This kind of equipment is becoming increasingly available to North American installers.

the local level, state and federal agencies and foundations might also be sources for support.

Yorktowne Square in Virginia, for example, described earlier in this chapter, is not a luxury community, and the price of a green roof at first appeared to put it out of reach. Jeanette Stewart, however, was active in various regional environmental groups and had seen grant opportunities applicable to green roof projects in their journals. She enlisted help from state and local agencies and secured an agreement from a local nonprofit to administer the funds. Her efforts yielded a $50,000 grant from the National Fish and Wildlife Foundation and a $29,000 grant from the Virginia Department of Conservation and Recreation. The extra money made the price of the green roof competitive with that of a conventional replacement.

Designing for stormwater performance

Beyond seeking to ensure that drainage is adequate for large storms but not so aggressive that plants are routinely stressed, green roof performance is rarely precisely calibrated in design. It's difficult to predict performance using existing stormwater design tools or models (EPA 2009a). The characteristics of the materials used in the assembly, including the growing medium

Benefits such as significant reductions in stormwater runoff are maximized when green roofs are installed on a large scale. This is most easily done when the best performance for the lowest cost can be readily calculated.

and drainage layer, will have a significant impact on a roof's stormwater performance. But designers can draw some useful conclusions from research and experience.

Flatter green roofs, for example, will generally retain more runoff than those with a steeper slope (Getter et al. 2007; Taylor 2008), and using an aggregate drainage layer rather than more transmissive synthetic sheets can improve retention (Taylor 2008). Based on early data, Charlie Miller and Robert Berghage say that longer flow paths on large green roofs appear to have a significantly positive impact on stormwater performance. Increasing the depth of medium can improve runoff retention (Van Woert et al. 2005; Wanielista et al. 2008), but the returns diminish after a certain point (Taylor 2008).

Some local stormwater codes prescribe or suggest a minimum depth for green roof medium and other design details. If stormwater management is important to your client but the project is not subject to this kind of regulation, some guidance can be obtained from stormwater manuals from jurisdictions with a similar climate.

The following discussion shows how factoring in stormwater performance can affect a project's bottom line.

Increasing medium depth works—up to a point

According to Robert Berghage of Penn State University's Center for Green Roof Research, the effect of deeper medium on annual or monthly water retention is more limited than it is for an individual storm because most storms are small—few will exceed the system's storage capacity—and much of the stormwater that runs off a green roof does so in the winter, when the roof remains wet.

On a flat green roof (slope also affects retention a great deal) the benefit is greatest as the depth increases from 1 to 5 inches (2.5 to 12.5 cm). Going from 1 to 2 percent up to 8 percent can make a significant difference, perhaps as much as 50 percent of the system's total storage capacity, depending on other variables. But the benefit becomes relatively smaller as the depth continues to increase beyond 5 inches (12.5 cm). The amount of water held in a specific slice of medium decreases rapidly with increasing depth from very shallow systems to deeper ones but the magnitude of the change diminishes as depth gets greater—

the relationship between water retention and medium depth is not linear.

With this in mind, consider the following hypothetical example. During a wet month, such as July in many parts of the United States, there might be nine precipitation events with the following characteristics: five storms with 0 to 0.5 inch (1.25 cm) of total precipitation, equaling 1.25 inches (3.1 cm); three storms with 0.25 to 1 inch (0.63 to 2.5 cm) of total precipitation, equaling 2.25 inches (5.6 cm); and one storm with 2.4 inches (6.0 cm) of total precipitation; bringing the total for the month to 5.9 inches (14.7 cm).

Assume that all of these storms are separated by three to five days, so the roof assembly can dry out between the storms. If a 2-inch (5-cm) roof can retain 0.6 inches (1.5 cm) on average, then retention for this month is about 3.4 inches (8.5 cm), or about 57 percent. If a 4-inch (10-cm) roof can retain about 1 inch (2.5 cm) on average for a given storm event, then in this example it will retain about 4.5 inches (11.25 cm) of the monthly rainfall, or 76 percent. If the depth of the medium is doubled to 8 inches (20 cm), it can retain about 1.75 inches (4.38 cm) of rain from a given event, or about 89 percent of the total.

Leaving aside all other roof costs, if the price of the medium is $144 per cubic yard, and a yard spread out 1 inch (2.5 cm) thick will cover 324 square feet (30 square meters), then the cost of medium per inch of depth is $0.44. The cost to retain 57 percent of rainfall for the month is $0.88, 76 percent is $1.78, and 89 percent is $3.52. That is, the cost to go from 0 to 57 percent retention is $0.88. A 19 percent increase in storage can be obtained for an additional $0.88, but the next 13 percent increase will cost an extra $1.76.

The calculation for a large storm is, of course, different. For a 2.4-inch (6-cm) rain event, 2 inches (5 cm) of medium for $0.88 retains only 25 percent of that storm. Four inches (10 cm) of medium for $1.78 retains 42 percent. Eight inches (20 cm) of medium for $3.52 retains 73 percent. But in most parts of North America, most rain falls in the form of small storms.

In the winter, the roof is wet much more of the time and so retains a smaller amount of any given storm, approximately 0.2 inch (0.5 cm) for a 2-inch (5-cm) roof, 0.3 inch (0.75 cm) for a

4-inch (10-cm) roof, and perhaps 0.4 inch (1 cm) for an 8-inch (20-cm) roof. So if you do the same calculations there is almost no return for going deeper.

The answer, then, to how much stormwater a green roof retains depends on how you ask the question. But a roof with 3 to 5 inches (7.5 to 12.5 cm) of medium, as is commonly promoted for stormwater management, seems to be a good compromise between cost and effect.

Green roof design paradigms: green roofs as amenity spaces

An amenity green roof is an aesthetic step up from a basic extensive green roof. It might include space for seating or gathering, or

Even a simple green roof assembly and plant palette can provide an attractive and comfortable amenity space if the building's loading capacity can accommodate people, furniture, and other accessories.

it might just serve to beautify a view out a window or from a neighboring building. Because this kind of design is so variable, it's difficult to generalize about its features. But an amenity green roof might include the following in some combination: a variety of plant species, possibly including herbaceous perennials, annuals, and grasses; a designed planting plan; mounded medium for different planting depths and microclimates; and walkways, patios, and seating if the building structure permits.

Amenity green roofs have several advantages over basic extensive green roofs. They have a more dynamic, colorful, and textural appearance. Their better looks and accessible space, if available, might enhance the value or marketability of the building. And additional medium depth might improve stormwater performance and energy savings. There are disadvantages to amenity green roofs, however, including higher cost and a possible need for a more complex assembly. More time, labor, and expertise are usually required to keep the design intact.

While it's easy to design a beautiful roof garden when you can use trees, shrubs, and colorful perennials, designing an extensive green roof for great looks requires some creativity and perhaps some attitude adjustment. An extensive green roof is never going to look like the Hanging Gardens of Babylon or Rockefeller Center. But the leap from a basic extensive green roof to one that offers a little bit more to its users is not always a great one.

For our purposes, "amenity" means going beyond pure function. An extensive green roof system can in some cases serve as a roof garden (albeit one without shrubs and trees). Extensive and intensive spaces can also be combined on a single roof to maximize green space while accommodating structural or budgetary constraints. And sometimes, an amenity is just an attractive view out a window.

Use an extensive green roof as a roof garden

While most extensive green roofs are not designed for regular access beyond that required for maintenance, if the building structure and budget allow for it, there is no reason that patios or at least walkways cannot be included in the design if there are areas of concentrated loading, allowing for greater visitation and use. Common green roof plants do not offer the same lushness or variation available on an intensive roof garden, but the extensive system is lighter and less expensive to install and maintain. It can serve as an attractive groundcover that keeps the space cooler and more pleasant than would an expanse of hardscape, while providing the same array of benefits.

When building a new, green headquarters in southeastern Pennsylvania, the leaders of the Dansko shoe company wanted accessible green roof space. But they did not want to sink a lot of resources into it. A traditional roof garden was not an option, says facilities manager Daria Payne. That would have required increasing the structural capability of the building and therefore required enhancements in the materials used to construct it. It would also have required more attention, in terms of money, la-

One of the green roofs on the Dansko headquarters is accessible to employees and visitors. A mix of succulents and drought-tolerant flowering plants were installed in 4 inches (10 cm) of growing medium laid over 2 inches (5 cm) of drainage aggregate. The system is lightweight, it provides good retention of stormwater runoff, and it requires little maintenance.

Above left: A few tough flowering perennials were included among the succulents to provide seasonal color.

Above right: A small area visible from the company's on-site retail store was designed to accommodate taller shrubs so shoppers can catch a glimpse of green.

bor for maintenance, and resources such as water, than they were willing to give.

While Payne and her colleagues wanted an amenity space for employees, their main objectives for the green roofs—there are three, including one small intensive space to accommodate taller plants and shrubs outside the retail area—were to manage stormwater and save energy. An extensive application, including on the accessible space on the highest roof with a patio and pergola, fit the bill nicely. It's neat and pretty, Payne says, and they can add a few planters if they want flowers or other foliage effects. "Part of sustainability is managing resources," says Payne. "We had other fish to fry than managing high-maintenance landscapes."

Plants on the accessible roof were installed as plugs in 4 inches (10 cm) of growing medium laid on 2 inches (5 cm) of drainage aggregate. A separate inaccessible roof was planted with cuttings on 2 inches (5 cm) of growing medium and 2 inches (5 cm) of drainage aggregate. The intensive retail roof has 6 inches (15 cm) of medium blended for semi-intensive use over 4 inches (10 cm) of aggregate. The drainage aggregate was also used as bedding material for the patio and edging pavers. All of the roofs, installed in early 2008, are functioning well and looking good, but the plugs on the accessible roof established extremely quickly during their first growing season, making the space almost instantly attractive.

Some Dansko visitors are from other organizations considering a green roof or roof garden. "They come in thinking, ugh, who wants just sedums? That's so boring," says Payne. "They want something sexier, like shrubs and grasses. Then they see our roof, and how little regular attention it needs, and almost everyone walks away with a new vision."

The design of this green roof at Penn State University makes it easy for students to study and maintain the plants.

Most of the plants on the roof are succulents, but one area had the capacity to allow a deeper system and a more diverse array of plants, including flowering perennials.

This green roof, on a post office facility in New York City, offers plenty of seating. Trees, growing in planters over strong support columns, will eventually provide shade. Keeping most of the roof design more basic helped to keep down costs while managing stormwater runoff and providing a large, low-maintenance planted area. Photograph by Linda McIntyre

A green roof on a classroom building at Penn State University features a similar design. A deck was built on an area with more concentrated loading. A deeper course of medium was also installed here so that different plants could be trialed and monitored by students, who also maintain the entire green roof. When loading capacity is not constrained, but the budget is, small deep areas for intensive planting can supplement a roof planted mostly with more common green roof succulents.

Expand the plant palette

The easiest way to give an extensive green roof a little bit more visual oomph is to tweak the planting palette. This can be as simple as overseeding a standard sedum planting.

Light weight was crucial on a 2008 residential retrofit project on the Hudson River in New York City. Installers Goode Green used less than 2 inches (5 cm) of growing medium over a membrane that required no separate root barrier. Sedum plugs and cuttings were planted, an obvious choice for this extreme environment. But to satisfy the client's love of bright colors, seeds of flowering plants such as *Dianthus barbatus*, *Papaver nudicaule*, and *Rudbeckia hirta* were oversown.

The green roof on this house on the Hudson River had to be thin and lightweight. Sedum plugs and cuttings were overseeded with wildflowers. Photograph courtesy of Goode Green

The client enjoys the colorful display, and the roof has been easy to maintain. Photograph courtesy of Goode Green

Flowering perennials such as *Campanula*, *Erigeron glaucus* and *Prunella vulgaris*, *Petrorhagia saxifraga*, *Talinum calycinum*, and *Dianthus* and *Allium* can do well in green roof systems.

The roof thrived in its first two growing seasons and the client was thrilled with its meadowy appearance. So much so, says Lisa Goode, that they plan to cut back the sedums a bit each spring to leave space for the wildflowers to bloom.

Adding depth to the system is another strategy. While a deeper course of growing medium will often support a more diverse range of plants, once you move beyond the workhorse hardy succulents, it becomes more difficult to generalize about appropriate species. Some colorful and drought-tolerant flowering plants, such as *Talinum calycinum* and *Allium*, are easily incorporated into a typical extensive plant palette, and some shallow-rooted herbaceous perennial species, such as *Petrorhagia, Dianthus, Phlox, Campanula, Teucrium, Potentilla, Achillea, Prunella, Viola*, and *Origanum*, can also be used on an extensive roof, depending on the regional climate and the exposure on the site. An irrigation system will further expand planting opportunities—as well as weed pressure.

When the historic Gimbels Department Store building in downtown Pittsburgh was under renovation after more than a decade of vacancy, the H. J. Heinz Company set its sights on the top floor for its executives. The offices had floor-to-ceiling windows, but the view they showed off—a black tar roof and brick parapet wall—left much to be desired. The building's new owner and their architects wanted to improve the space with a roof garden. But while structural capacity was not an issue for the sturdy building, the budget was. The architects suggested a green roof, which in 2001 was a somewhat obscure solution.

The system, designed by Roofscapes, comprised 3 inches (7.5 cm) of growing medium over 2 inches (5 cm) of drainage aggregate. This depth, and the protection afforded by the 8-foot (2.4-m) parapet wall, allowed a bit of leeway in the planting design. The team took advantage of this by developing a long plant list, including a variety of grasses and flowering perennials in addition to more than a dozen hardy succulents. Flowering species include *Campanula rotundifolia, Phlox subulata, Dianthus deltoides*, and *Potentilla neumanniana*.

Plugs, along with seeds of some species, were planted in drifts to show off contrasts in texture and color. Because the long-term maintenance contract provides for only one annual

While the planting design is relatively simple and carefree, this building's parapet wall offers some extra shelter to support more flowering plants and some grasses. Photograph courtesy of Roofscapes

visit from the contractor, however, the roof's appearance has grown less formal and more meadowy. There's a lot of color in spring from the perennials, and the grasses add height and texture. The system requires little intervention: It has never been irrigated, and the maintenance routine involves removal of aggressive weeds, replanting of exposed areas, and a soil analysis. A light dressing of slow-release fertilizer was applied for the first time in 2008.

Sometimes, rather than imposing a design on a roof, it's easier to let the roof guide your design and plant palette. On an

Above: In spring, the roof, which is visible to the Heinz company's top executives, resembles a flowery meadow. Photograph courtesy of Roofscapes

Left: Microclimates have a large impact on plant performance. Shade cast by the storage shed on this roof probably accounts for the proliferation of alliums in this area.

unirrigated green roof, microclimates in sheltered areas provide opportunities to use plants that struggle in more exposed spaces. "I'm skeptical that in an exposed area you can have that much effect by varying thickness," says engineer and designer Charlie Miller. "I think you really have to focus on sheltered areas. I would put the deep medium in the most sheltered areas and grow perennials and grasses. But it has to be both, unless you're willing to irrigate."

Articulate design forms with plant species

Hardy succulents can be planted in single-species groups to produce simple design effects on an extensive green roof. Maintaining bright lines of demarcation will require more maintenance than is usually required on an extensive roof. Usually these lines will blur over time as different species wax and wane depending on conditions and the seasons.

For this purpose, qualities such as color, height, and texture are secondary. The key characteristic for plants in an articulated design is persistence. If planted in single-species swaths, plants with a long dormant period will leave areas of exposed medium that can erode or host weeds. Species that produce a lot of viable seed should also be avoided if maintaining a planting design is

Plugs of green roof plants can be planted in single-species swaths to realize geometric or fanciful designs. Make sure the installation crew knows which plants belong in which spaces.

important. Choosing the wrong species will increase the maintenance load for the client.

After installation, an articulated design using plugs will not have a filled-in, bedded-out look right away. The plugs will still need the usual amount of time to establish, though different species can establish at noticeably different rates, which can affect maintenance routines. If you want faster establishment, you can increase the density of plugs. While buying more plants will cost

Left and below left: Different plant species will establish at different rates, and their appearances will change according to the seasons.

Below: It's difficult to establish and maintain a very strong geometric planting design with species that grow at very different rates. Keeping the design well articulated also requires a lot of maintenance.

Pregrown modules, planted with different species, can be used to achieve and maintain a strong planting design. Modules without exposed plastic edges provide a neater, more seamless look.

a bit more, the price increase might not be significant, because you will already be paying to transport plants and get them on the roof. Paying a little bit more up front can also reduce the effort required for maintenance, because less medium will be exposed. For more information on specifying plugs, see "Specifying common green roof plants" in chapter 2.

Another way to achieve uniform single-species sections quickly is to use pregrown modules. The shape of the modules, obviously, will limit the shape of the designs, and modules are an expensive option. But this approach will reduce the level of maintenance necessary to maintain the integrity of the design, because the establishment phase will have occurred off-site. If the modules are plastic, as most of them are, they will also keep the plants from blurring the lines by spreading—though some species can self-seed into other modules.

Sculpt berms

Mounding medium is an easy way to give a green roof some topography and expand the plant palette. Berms give more planting options both by providing a deeper root zone and by creating microclimates in sheltered areas. Plants along the ridge of the berm, such as taller grasses, can also provide shade and shelter

Mounds of deeper medium can support larger plants and create sheltered microclimates as well as visually interesting topography.

Taller grasses can help exaggerate the effect of mounded areas.
Photograph by Linda McIntyre

for other species. In addition, they can hide, or at least draw the eye away from, unsightly features such as air vents and HVAC equipment.

If the weight of the assembly is not an issue or on areas with concentrated loading opportunities, such as over structural beams, the medium can simply be mounded according to the desired shape. Some designers use moisture retention mats for extra stabilization of mounded areas. The growing medium can also be laid over a Styrofoam base if weight is a concern.

All-medium berms will provide a deeper root zone, but especially with higher mounds keeping the plants well watered during establishment is important. Before roots are well established, water moves quickly downward through the assembly and therefore away from the small root zone of a newly planted plug. Because creating berms is a tool for expanding a roof's plant list, it's likely that the plants along its ridge will be less tolerant of dry conditions than hardy succulents. These sections of the roof will require a little bit more attention than areas that are not mounded, but it's a small commitment for a potentially great impact.

Attend to details

Small, inexpensive, well-chosen details can enhance a green roof that will be seen or visited regularly. Be creative with paved and unplanted areas. Make sure, of course, that selected materials meet the relevant requirements—stone in nonvegetated areas, for example, must be heavy enough to resist wind pressure, and hardscape or paving must support enough weight and work in combination with substrate materials.

Embrace the dynamic

When working with a more diverse plant palette or a more sophisticated planting design, it's important to keep some things in mind. Just as they will at grade, plants will respond to conditions on a roof in different ways. In any multispecies planting, the percentages of various species won't remain stable but will wax and wane depending on the season, temperature, rainfall, and

other variables. Some plants will adapt very well and spread quickly, others will take longer, and still others might never fully adjust and gradually die out. Some will disperse a lot of viable seed and multiply.

Attempting to maintain a consistent planting design usually requires a lot of work. Some species are easy to control by regular hand-pulling. Sometimes this kind of maintenance can be mitigated in design by using well-behaved species and building in features such as nonvegetated gravel strips to keep the lines of the planting plan intact. But sometimes it's worthwhile to let plants migrate to areas with conditions they prefer and enjoy the changes.

Above left: Attractive stones can be used to enhance nonvegetated areas around penetrations.

Above right: Strong metal grates can support foot traffic while letting light through to plants below. When the plants grow tall enough, walking on the grates breaks off the ends of succulents, producing cuttings that root and grow into new plants.

A green roof, even one planted only with succulents, will look different in different seasons. A green roof in Maryland in January, February, March, April, May, and June.

The same roof in July, August, September, October, November, and December.

The look of a green roof will also change from year to year, even after establishment. An unirrigated green roof on Alice Paul Hall at Swarthmore College in Pennsylvania just after installation in 2004 and in the early summer of 2005, 2007, 2008, and 2009. As this roof illustrates, weather conditions play a large role. The summer of 2008 was warm and dry, but the flowers came right back in the cool and rainy summer of 2009.

Green roof design paradigms: specialty green roofs

Rethinking the rooftop as a space for growing plants opens up alluring possibilities. If you are going to be planting up there, why settle for humble succulents when you can restore some native flora, provide wildlife habitat, harvest fruits and vegetables, or walk barefoot through the grass? The advantages of such specialty green roofs include potentially higher ecological output for some landscape types, social benefits from community gardening/food production, and walkable amenity space in the case of a lawn roof. There are, however, some disadvantages. The relationship of benefits to inputs is not always clear. These types of roofs are more difficult to design: Specialist knowledge, deeper medium, and irrigation are usually needed for this kind of project. In addition, their maintenance requires more labor, resources, and expertise.

Turf grass and other non-succulent plants can be grown on a green roof, but such designs require careful design and extra maintenance.

Compared to a conventional green roof, it's usually a lot more difficult to build and maintain such specialty green roofs. Sedums and other hardy succulents are the easiest and most cost-effective plants to use on a green roof. They are commercially available, inexpensive, easy to install, and likely to survive if given proper attention during the establishment period. In most situations these plants will spread and provide the vegetated cover necessary for optimal roof performance. Over the longer term, maintenance of this type of roof, especially if done regularly, is neither difficult nor prohibitively expensive. A roof planted primarily with hardy succulents can accommodate other species in protected areas for a more varied appearance and increased habitat value.

It's possible to grow native plants, provide habitat, enjoy lawn spaces, or grow food on a roof, though some of these paradigms should still be considered experimental. But the design process for these projects, as well as the green roof assembly itself, will be more complex. It will often require specialized experience and a longer timeframe. Maintenance will almost always require more effort and more expertise. The designer has to be fully aware of the implications of this kind of approach and make the client aware as well. Installing roofs like this will add to the body of green roof knowledge and foster innovation, but everyone involved with the project should be clear that this is pioneering, not proven, work.

Native Plants on Green Roofs

The growing interest in designing with native plants has generated interest in using these species on green roofs. It can, in some situations, be done successfully. But selecting and obtaining the right plants can be difficult and time-consuming, and the site specificity of this approach means that little guidance can be taken from successful examples in other regions.

Native plants are popular in gardens

Planting trends have an impact beyond the garden, and in recent years interest among gardeners in native plants has grown substantially. Factors contributing to this rise include concern about

Native plants such as *Monarda fistulosa* can be grown on some green roofs, but the design must accommodate these plants. Often this will mean deeper growing medium and a built-in irrigation system.

the impact of invasive exotic plants, the perceived ability of native plant species to thrive in local conditions without excessive maintenance, and the desire to provide habitat for local wildlife and insects.

These same laudable desires and concerns and the LEED program's emphasis on vaguely defined "native or adapted" plants have prompted some designers to specify native plants on green roofs. Often, however, such plants, even when they are properly identified and available in the marketplace, struggle in the harsh conditions on a roof. It's possible, in some situations, to use native plants successfully on green roof projects, but the decision to do so should not be taken lightly.

Even in a garden at grade, using native plants to improve ecological function and provide habitat is not simply a matter of choosing a few natives off the shelf of the local nursery and adding them to a plant list. There's nothing wrong with using species broadly defined as native to enhance a garden's appearance or attractiveness to local wildlife or to create a more lush and flowery green roof designed to sustain such a plant palette. But restoration ecology goes far beyond horticulture and requires knowledge of biology, soil science, climate, hydrology, and how the characteristics of a site interact (Simmons et al. 2007). On a roof, there's nothing to restore.

Native plants cannot necessarily live on a roof

Applying these principles on a green roof adds additional complications. A roof assembly capable of supporting a variety of herbaceous plants is likely to be more complex and expensive than that for a simple extensive roof. Deeper growing medium and an irrigation program will almost always be needed, as will careful long-term maintenance and management by properly trained staff.

This reality has to be balanced against the project objectives. If the building owner wants a certain level of ecosystem service from the building, using native plants might theoretically appear to improve that level of service, given the widespread belief that native plants are carefree choices that will automatically thrive. But if the inputs required for a native plant palette exceed the benefit they provide, then the owner might be better off with a simpler approach.

A green roof in Washington, D.C., was planted with natives but was not designed to support those plants. The growing medium was only a few inches deep and included a lot of large coarse particles that shed water quickly. No irrigation system was built in. Almost all of the native species died, and weeds quickly colonized the bare medium.

The owner, deeply committed to sustainability but lacking green roof experience, was not fully informed of the maintenance

If the design does not accommodate specified native plants, the roof can become a bank of invasive weed seeds.

required, especially for a roof planted with flowering perennials. The small on-site maintenance crew, also charged with caring for the at-grade landscape and turf playing field, was not trained to care for the roof. The owner is exploring ways to eliminate the weed bank and replant the roof with a more appropriate plant palette.

Selecting appropriate native species for a rooftop project is a complex undertaking that requires specialized scientific exper-

The design of this green roof could not support the specified native plants. Photograph by Linda McIntyre

The growing medium on this roof has a particle distribution that cannot support plants that need a lot of water, and it's not deep enough to support deep root systems.

Without irrigation, native plants on green roofs can look unattractive during dry spells.

If you want to use native species on a green roof, seek out plants native to your region. These native plants have been used on extensive green roof projects based on analysis of local reference populations:

Armeria maritima

Asclepias fascicularis

Asclepias tuberosa

Carex pensylvanica

Eschscholzia californica

Fragaria chiloensis

Lasthenia californica

Layia platyglossa

Lespedeza cuneata

Lupinus bicolor

Monarda fistulosa

Plantago erecta

Prunella vulgaris

Solidago odora

Sorghastrum nutans

tise. In addition, it's often difficult to source native species, especially in the juvenile state best suited to green roof planting. Custom propagation will add to the cost and the timeline of the project. The roof will almost certainly require more maintenance to keep the plants alive. Finally, the aesthetics of a native plant palette might not fit the owner's notion of either a lush, flowery garden or even a more basic but tidy-looking green roof. All of these issues should be addressed early in the design phase so that everyone involved in the project—designers and client alike—are aware of the implications of this ambitious design choice.

Just what *is* a native plant?

This is a surprisingly difficult and complex question. Plants know no state or national boundaries. Calling a plant "native to North America" doesn't say much, because the continent includes areas of tundra, tropical rainforest, desert, and grassland, among others. Thinking in terms of bioregions or ecoregions—places with similar geology, topography, climate, soil, hydrology, and plant and animal life—is more useful for this purpose, but even within bioregions there's a lot of diversity. In addition, it can be difficult to apply these concepts on urban and suburban sites, where the qualities that define bioregions have been drastically changed by human intervention.

Thinking in terms of bioregions is even more difficult on a rooftop. Plants must be able to survive both inundation and prolonged drought (often without irrigation) and extreme heat and cold. The growing medium usually used on green roofs for its light weight and free-draining properties is low in organic matter and cannot sustain complex biota in the way that soil does. While there are some situations in nature, such as cliff faces, that bear some resemblance to the urban built environment including green roofs (Lundholm 2006), it's not always possible to find an analog anywhere near your site.

Consider using natives in some situations

Research and experience in the field in both Europe and North America shows that hardy succulents such as sedums are the easiest to grow on a roof (Monterusso et al. 2005). But if you are willing to commit to a more complex, expensive, and mainte-

The concave roof of the Ballard Library in Seattle is planted with native grasses. Native plants on a roof can work in some situations when the building owner is fully apprised of the pros and cons.

nance-intensive project, there are reasons to consider using native plants.

As in gardens at grade, the potential for restoring biodiversity using native plants on roofs is in theory enormous, and the small but growing body of research on using a broader plant palette and planting roofs to attract wildlife, most of it from Europe, is encouraging (Brenneisen 2006; Köhler 2006). Using native plants to improve the ecological function of green roofs is also a tantalizing, though mostly unrealized, possibility. Native herbaceous plants and grasses suitable for a roof planting would probably have greater leaf area than sedums, and therefore could provide additional evapotranspiration and a better cooling function for the building. Increased biomass at the root level might take up captured stormwater from the medium faster than the shallow roots of sedums, and the water quality of any runoff

The green roof on the California Academy of Sciences is planted with a carefully selected native plant palette.

might be higher owing to more effective filtration. But there are not yet hard data to support these hypotheses.

Aesthetically the use of native species cuts both ways. On one hand, some feel that the low profile and limited variation of sedums and other hardy succulents lack visual excitement, whereas natives can offer a greater variety of color, texture, and structure. On the other hand, most native plant green roofs are not going to be a pretty, flowery garden most of the time. Many native species are not very showy themselves, and their messy look during dormancy, which sometimes extends over a long period, might be a negative for some.

One of the best reasons to use native plants is for research and education. The green roof on the California Academy of Sciences, with its seven crowning hills echoing those of its San Francisco home, has made a big splash. Its novel and complex

The roof is used for research and education and is highly maintained to preserve a neat and attractive appearance year-round.

design put this green roof in a class by itself, but the process of choosing and caring for the native plants that populate it offers lessons for anyone considering tackling such a project.

The architect, Renzo Piano, wanted a smooth, monolithic look. That low, ground-hugging appearance is typical of many *Sedum* species that are commonly used on green roofs. But the academy wanted the roof planted with California natives to foster research projects, and they wanted plants that looked good virtually all of the time to keep the roof's many visitors engaged.

A lot of care went into choosing the plant palette for the roof area and a more diverse native exhibition garden around an accessible observation deck. Frank Almeda, a senior botanist at the California Academy of Sciences, and Paul Kephart of Rana Creek, an ecological restoration firm with a wholesale native plant nursery, tested about thirty species, looking for plants that could stand up to the harsh conditions on the roof (especially the hills) and provide habitat for wildlife including the Bay checkerspot (*Euphydryas editha bayensis*) and San Bruno elfin (*Callophrys mossii bayensis*) butterflies.

An early mockup frightened the architect with its unkempt appearance, "like a tumbleweed on stilts," says John Loomis of SWA Group, the landscape architect for the project. Ultimately four perennials were selected: *Prunella vulgaris*, *Fragaria chiloensis*, *Armeria maritima*, and *Sedum spathulifolium*. To provide sufficient cover for the opening of the new building in October 2008, five annuals were added to the mix: *Eschscholzia californica*, *Lupinus bicolor*, *Lasthenia californica*, *Plantago erecta*, and *Layia platyglossa*.

The California Academy of Sciences is following through on its research and education objectives. In addition to frequent tours and interpretive signs, the comings and goings of flora and fauna on the roof are closely monitored. Students from San Francisco State University are taking monthly samples of insects, and interns are working with Almeda to monitor an empty test plot on the roof's west side to track which plant species show up on the roof without intervention. Eventually academy researchers hope to introduce the threatened butterflies on the roof; the exhibition garden was designed with a lot of larval host plants, such as *Asclepias fascicularis*, but they take a couple of years to mature and become useful to the butterflies.

When your client wants natives, determine the underlying objective

In practice, the use of natives rather than a more traditional green roof plant palette is sometimes dictated by the client rather than the designer. If you are on the design or construction side of the project, it's important that you and your client agree on objectives and on how you intend to define "native" for the purposes of your project.

Objectives that might drive such a choice include the desire to use the roof for research (especially if the project is affiliated with a school or other institution); to attract wildlife (exactly what kind of wildlife and the implications of insects or animals on the roof should be discussed at length among the client, design team, and maintenance team); and to "do the right thing" with respect to the environment. The two former goals will drive plant selection in specific ways—creating the sort of habitat to attract particular pollinators, for example, or ground-nesting birds reliant on taller plants for food sources for their chicks (Brenneisen 2006).

The last goal is too vague to be of use and would have to be refined, perhaps into a more traditional green roof plant list with some additional species used in sheltered areas or parts of the roof where deeper medium could be used. A frank discussion with the client might also calm fears that a more tried-and-true approach would somehow upset the ecology of the site. While sedums and other hardy succulents establish and spread quickly when conditions are favorable, the vast majority of these species are extremely unlikely to escape cultivation and spread into natural areas. Aggressive varieties such as *Sedum sarmentosum* are rarely used on green roof projects and are recommended only for projects for which it will be the only species used or that will be subject to frequent regular maintenance.

If, after understanding the degree of difficulty, your client wants native plants on the project, the design process will involve some steps not associated with more basic design paradigms.

Sometimes objectives such as attracting pollinators can be achieved by incorporating a few non-native species, such as this *Delosperma* 'Beaufort West', in protected areas. This is an easier, lower maintenance approach than a design comprising all native species.

Identify appropriate plant communities

Most serious native plant advocates and ecologists advise using plant communities, as opposed to a more random group of species, in restoration projects, gardens, and specialty projects such as green roofs. But as with native plants, the concept is a bit more complicated than it might appear at first. The thinking on plant communities, even among scientists, has evolved over time from notions of distinct and discrete entities to those of a less-tightly integrated group of species interacting along a continuum to a dynamic and fluid community influenced by human, environmental, and other disturbances (McCarthy 2008). In addition, the native flora of North America does not include a lot of succulents, especially those with a spreading habit, which are the plants best adapted to use on green roofs.

Given this complexity, those who want to work with native plant communities on a roof should work closely with scientists

The plants on this green roof, on the Ethical Culture Fieldston School in the Bronx, were selected by scientists at Columbia University from nearby reference communities. Photograph by Kinne Stires

who are deeply familiar with the local ecology and flora. A native plant roof at the Ethical Culture Fieldston School in the Bronx, New York, illustrates how such a project might work. Originally, the Columbia University team that drove this project planned to plant the entire vegetated area on both levels of the green roof with sedums. But Matt Palmer, a plant ecologist from the university, contacted Stuart Gaffin of Columbia's Center for Climate Systems Research and wanted to get involved. Palmer had only recently learned about green roofs but was inspired by the possibility of restoring wildlife habitat to urban areas. He also told Gaffin that a limited plant palette, as originally envisaged, would be boring for the biology teachers who would be using the lower roof as a teaching tool.

Palmer drew up a plant list for the 1500 square foot (140 square meter) lower roof using indigenous herbaceous plant communities from the region as model systems. (The less-accessible

Fieldston students use the roof as a classroom while learning about local ecosystems. Photograph by Laura Dickinson

upper roof has a thinner profile and is planted with sedums.) To find plants that would survive on a rooftop environment, he looked for communities dominated by native grasses and perennials that grow in thin soil under lots of light.

Using information from the New York Natural Heritage Program, Palmer focused on two: the Hempstead Plains, a small remnant prairie (the only such landscape in New York State) on Long Island, and the Rocky Summit grasslands in the nearby Hudson River Valley. He chose a mix of broadleaf plants such as *Solidago odora* and *Asclepias tuberosa*, grasses such as *Carex pensylvanica* and *Sorghastrum nutans*, and legumes such as *Lespedeza cuneata* to fix nitrogen in the growing medium, increasing its fertility.

Medium, 6 inches (15 cm) deep in most areas, was mounded in some areas on this roof to try to accommodate deeper root systems, but Gaffin says that he's not sure whether this was done in a rigorous enough fashion as some of these areas have suffered erosion and lost their structure. Plants were installed at the direction of the scientists in both grid and randomized patterns.

Fieldston students are doing insect, biomass, and survivorship surveys. Except for some of the grasses, they were reporting over 90 percent survival as of autumn 2008, a year after it was planted. Gaffin plans to monitor temperatures here, as he is on the upper roof and other green roofs around the city. Laura Dickinson, a Columbia graduate student, has developed curriculum lesson plans around the project. Sixth-grade students studied species mapping, the benefits of green roofs, ecosystem dynamics, and the functions of different plants. Every year, students hold an open house on the roof for visitors.

Find a source to supply or grow your plants

If you follow this template for choosing native plants for a green roof project, you might well find it difficult or impossible to find the plants at a commercial nursery. The team on the Fieldston project had access to New York City's Greenbelt Native Plant Center, a greenhouse and nursery owned by the Department of Parks and Recreation that provides native plants for restoration projects undertaken by the city. Even so, Palmer had to adjust his list according to what the nursery was able to grow, and some plants were not available until the roof's second growing season.

Researchers elsewhere have run into similar difficulties. According to Mark Simmons, an ecologist at the Lady Bird Johnson Wildflower Center in Austin, while there are about 5200 plants native to Texas, only about fifty are available as live material and about fifty more as seeds. Only a small subset of these might have potential for use on green roofs. Though the center and other institutions are conducting research and trials, there is at this point no definitive list of native plants that work on green roofs. The sort of analysis required for this approach means that, for the foreseeable future, each native plant green roof is in essence its own research project.

For private-sector projects, custom propagation might be the only way to get the native plants you want. This will add to the cost of the project, and it will take longer to get the plants. Expect to factor in as much as a year for a grower to find the appropriate seeds and grow enough plants.

Using plants that have not been tried on green roofs also introduces additional elements of uncertainty to the project. The selected plants might not perform well over time and are unlikely to be covered by a warranty. Replacement is expensive, and new species will have to be found for spaces formerly inhabited by poor performers. Without aggressive maintenance, some species (often grasses on native roofs) will eventually dominate and the roof's appearance can change dramatically. Clients should be made fully aware of these potential difficulties in advance to avoid disappointment and recrimination.

Understand that without a serious and sustained maintenance program, the look of the roof will change dramatically

Preserving the plant palette on the California Academy of Sciences' roof, in keeping with the academy's aesthetic requirements and habitat objectives, has been required constant, vigilant, and skilled maintenance. Succession and seasonality are difficult to square with those goals. Visitors also arrive at the roof with high and specific expectations, because a movie in the planetarium shows images of the roof shot after a seeding of *Eschscholzia californica*. Since the other plants have established, however, the poppies cannot self-seed in the dense cover. Alan Good, the academy's landscape exhibits supervisor, has been adding poppies propagated from stubs, hoping to add a bit more color and diversity and give visitors what they came to see.

About a year and a half after the plants were installed on the roof, the distribution of the four perennials, each planted at the same rate of coverage, was hardly equivalent. *Prunella vulgaris*

Appropriate native species were chosen and properly installed on this green roof. But when this building was sold, the new owner did not want to put effort or resources into maintenance, and the plants died. Photograph of roof with living plants courtesy of Mark Simmons

had taken over about 70 percent of the roof. *Fragaria chiloensis* was fairly plentiful (Good says this is the first time he has ever seen this plant, a strawberry that spreads by runners, outcompeted), but there were few *Armeria maritima* and *Sedum spathulifolium* plants in evidence. High urea content in the growing medium might have compromised the establishment of the latter two species. Paul Kephart, who designed the biodegradable modules in which the plants were installed, says that was not consistent with Rana Creek's specification and was the result of a substitution by a contractor.

While the plants were selected for relatively low water and nutrient requirements, the demand for year-round good looks and a relatively diverse plant palette means that the irrigation and fertilization currently used on the roof will probably continue into the foreseeable future. That's the only way to maintain species diversity and preserve the roof's colorful appearance. The irrigation also prevents the plants from going into drought response and shriveling up or dying back completely. Good and others at the academy hope to educate the public about the true nature of the California landscape and gradually move away from the year-round lush green imperative, but that's a long-term plan.

The owners of another green roof took a very different approach. At the Aquascape headquarters in St. Charles, Illinois,

The plants on the Aquascape headquarters in St. Charles, Illinois, were given a head start with irrigation, then the landscape was left to evolve naturally.

the 130,000 square foot (12,090 square meter) roof was planted in 2005 with prairie natives selected and custom-propagated by a local nursery. An irrigation system helped the plants establish, but the company is planning to suspend its use after five years (this plant palette requires a longer establishment phase than hardy succulents would) except during extremely dry periods. If the plants struggle, Aquascape will resume regular watering. At the end of the first two growing seasons, a maintenance crew using weed trimmers cut back the plants to a couple of inches and carried off the detritus. The program was suspended after the third season, but can be reinstated if needed.

At first, the roof had a colorful flowery look, but soon the grasses outcompeted the flowering plants. The colors are now subdued, the grasses brown off at times, and the roof, with its exuberant unmanicured texture, blends in well with the at-grade landscape. The owner's understanding of the early effort necessary to promote good establishment and the reality of succession and seasonality with less maintenance over time made this project a success. It's not a real prairie restoration, and nobody pretends it is. Forces that act on real prairies, such as grazing animals and periodic fires, are not going to happen on this roof. But it's a regionally appropriate, relatively low-maintenance landscape that saves the company money and makes its employees proud.

Understand that each native plant green roof is unique

While research continues, there are few native plant roofs in the field that offer useful lessons. Many of those that exist are too new for us to judge their success, while industry pioneers learn by trial and error. Because "native" is, in the scientific sense, such a place-based quality, it will likely be difficult to draw conclusions that apply on a basis beyond the regional or local.

Benchmarks on which research and monitoring are focused include the stability of plant communities over time; the relationships between medium depth, fertility, succession, irrigation, and weed pressure; how the ecological function of native plants compares to that of traditional green roof plants; and any impact on the rate of stormwater discharge and the water quality of runoff. The data bear watching, and the possibilities are exciting. But a native plant green roof will always be more difficult to design, specify, and manage than one using mostly tried-and-true plants.

Green roofs as wildlife habitat

Some people assume that all green roofs function as excellent wildlife habitat, and some believe that using native plants on a green roof makes that roof a substitute for habitat at grade. The reality is much more complicated.

While any green roof, or even a ballast roof with weeds growing among the stones, will usually attract birds and insects, it's impossible to replicate at-grade habitat on the roof of a building. Similarly, a green roof, while offering an environment vastly superior to that of a black roof or parking lot in a densely built city, is not a replacement for open space destroyed by development. Designing a green roof for habitat is a complex undertaking that implicates virtually every aspect of the above-membrane assembly, not just the plant palette.

The European experience offers some lessons: you can replicate, but not recreate, habitat

Most of the research and field work on this subject have been done in Europe, where green roofs are common in some coun-

Most research on green roofs as habitat for specific species has been done in Europe. This study plot of Stephan Brenneisen revealed that different substrates and physical conditions are necessary to provide bird habitats on green roofs.

tries and a strong conservation ethos exists among many citizens. While projects in Europe show that design for habitat can be successful, it also demonstrates how complicated it is to achieve that success.

"Most ecologists try to *recreate* habitat," says Dusty Gedge, a United Kingdom–based wildlife consultant specializing in green roofs. "But that's the wrong approach at the roof level. You are replicating the *characteristics* of what was at grade—substrate, vegetation, and so on—within the context of a roof, which is a very different environment to that at grade." Gedge has spent years experimenting with what he calls "accoutrements"—logs, stones, wads of balled-up hay—that can provide shade, windbreaks, shelter, and nesting habitat for invertebrate species that populate dry, low-nutrient soils. This kind of roof, which can have swaths of bare substrate along with planted areas, is often called a "brown roof."

Establishing biodiversity will require some management

When Gedge began his roof-based conservation efforts, back in the 1990s, he assumed that simply putting rubble found on site up on the roof during construction and allowing volunteer plants to colonize the rubble would replicate the characteristics of the vacant land under development. Such sites are of significant conservation interest in the United Kingdom because they have provided habitat for protected bird species such as the black redstart (Gedge 2003). But Gedge found that this self-colonization approach did not work well in practice: desirable plants did not make the jump to roof level, but invasive species such as *Buddleia davidii*, which can cause serious damage to the building, came in droves.

Vary the depth and composition of the substrate and add accoutrements

Fortunately Gedge and his colleagues at the London Biodiversity Partnership happened upon the work of Stephan Brenneisen of Basel University in Switzerland. Brenneisen had done research confirming the value of green roofs for avian species such as the black redstart as well as mid-trophic invertebrates such as spiders and beetles, whose presence is a good indicator of biodiversity. In his research, Brenneisen had found that varying the depth of the substrate increased the number of rare invertebrates (Brenneisen 2003); coincidentally the black redstart also prefers an environment with varied topography.

Gedge began working with varying depths of substrate ranging from 3.5 to 6 inches (8.8 to 15 cm). He also began trying different compositions, using commercial substrates of varying sieve sizes as well as sand and boulders, mounding the material

Using substrates of different sizes can help foster biodiversity.

Logs and other accoutrements can provide shelter.

in some places to provide shelter for nesting and other activities. Plants were selected to perform in the different microclimates, engage desired species, and provide food or shelter. He also found that allowing the substrate to rest, exposed, on the site fosters better replication of local biodiversity by promoting the buildup of local seeds and colonization by nonaerial insects that cannot make it up to the roof after installation (Gedge 2003).

Expertise is necessary for fine-tuning

Designing a roof for habitat requires deep and specific knowledge of the needs of the species you are seeking to attract. For example, Gedge says species such as crested larks will look for areas of denser grass for nesting. A roof near an estuary might include bands of sand to attract shorebirds such as plovers. These birds will also need water to attract midges and other food sources, which can be provided by adding some space for ephemeral ponds. Otherwise, newborn chicks of these species will starve.

Tried-and-true green roof plants have a place

Gedge says commonly used green roof plants such as sedums can help support the rooftop ecosystem early in its lifetime, bringing in moisture that helps forbs and seeds of nectar-producing plants

Succulent plants can be used as placeholders while other species establish.

to grow, acting as placeholders for species that take longer to establish, and providing a tiny microclimate. But after five years, sedums will usually move out to thin, more exposed areas on the periphery of the roof. He and his colleagues are relaxed about a plant's origin, but they do avoid plants such as the common vetch (*Vicia sativa*), which might be attractive to wildlife (it attracts aphids, which in turn attract rare house sparrows in London) but spreads so aggressively it ultimately reduces the diversity on a roof.

Even a brown roof will need maintenance

Maintaining this sort of roof is about observation and adjustment. The tasks will have to be matched with the requirements of the desired species, such as preservation of bare areas or the keeping in check of sheltering tall grasses. As with any green roof, weeding will be the primary focus for the first year or two. Gedge says that in his experience many of these roofs become fairly self-sustaining after about three years. But that might not be the case in other regions, with different climate conditions and weed pressure.

Early information from North American green roofs is also encouraging

This kind of species-targeting habitat roof is rare in North America. But early research indicates that, regardless of intent, green roofs here—even very thin extensive roofs planted only with hardy succulents—have a surprisingly high level of species diversity for insects, spiders, and birds. In urban areas, simple extensive roofs can serve as useful stopovers during migration (Coffman and Waite 2009). As more green roofs are built, this area is ripe for more research.

Green roof as kitchen garden

It's always easier and more economical to grow vegetables and other food crops at grade. But on a small scale, and with attention to fertility requirements, irrigation, and maintenance, food can grow on a green roof. Usually this approach will require a deeper intensive system. Some designers, however, have success-

Above left: Beehives can be placed on green roofs for honey production.

Above right: Most rooftop kitchen gardens, such as this one in Chicago, have at least 18 inches (45 cm) of medium and an irrigation system.

Right: Some, however, are designed more along extensive green roof lines. This roof in Brooklyn uses 6 inches (15 cm) of growing medium, with extra organic matter blended in. Photograph courtesy of Goode Green

fully used an extensive system, with mounded areas and extra organic matter, to create an urban potager. In an inner-city environment, spaces like these can function as community gardens and settings for educational programs for children who have little access to farms and larger gardens.

Green roofs planted with turf-grass usually need a deeper course of growing medium and an irrigation system. Photograph courtesy of Roofscapes

Lawn on a roof

Turf might seem a surprising choice as a green roof plant, because it requires so much maintenance even at grade to provide the manicured swath of green homeowners expect. But when people live in apartments and condominiums rather than single-family houses, the roof might be the only accessible outdoor space. The high evapotranspiration rate of grass keeps the area cool and pleasant. Green roof growing medium, with its coarse mineral particles, stands up well to compression from foot traffic.

A green roof laid with lawn will require a deeper layer of growing medium—at least 6 inches (15 cm) for areas with little foot traffic, 8 inches (20 cm) for those with more frequent traffic, and 10 inches (25 cm) for heavy traffic. A permanent irrigation system is almost always required. Using harvested rainwater or other nonpotable sources can limit the environmental impact of a lawn roof.

Special design considerations and challenges

Some situations will require particular attention during the design phase. Green roofs can be installed in arid climates, on slopes, and in exposed or shaded sites, but the design, installation, and maintenance of such projects is usually more complex.

Irrigation

Sometimes irrigation will be necessary for a viable, long-lived green roof, but often it will come down to preference. Owners and designers should consider all of the pros and cons when deciding whether to include an irrigation system.

Permanent irrigation can be unnecessary or even counterproductive

Extensive green roofs in temperate climates usually do not require permanent irrigation. But, depending on weather conditions, some supplemental watering after planting is often necessary to make sure plants establish quickly and their roots have access to moisture, which moves quickly down the assembly. A water supply should be available for this kind of irrigation, and the maintenance team should know where it is. A spigot located at the roof level, designed to deliver water at adequate pressure, will make watering during establishment easier (Luckett 2009a).

Once the plants are off to a good start on a roof planted with sedums and other hardy succulents, regular irrigation, other than during extreme dry spells, can be counterproductive. In addition to conserving water and money, withholding supplemental water promotes longevity on an extensive green roof by fostering a more stable plant community and reduces maintenance because weeds are less likely to thrive in a low-water, low-nutrient environment (Miller 2009b).

But on some projects permanent irrigation makes sense

As is usually the case with green roofs, there are exceptions to the rule of thumb. Green roof engineer and designer Charlie Miller cites the following as reasons to irrigate a green roof: to support a project in an arid climate, to support a specific plant palette, and to optimize evapotranspiration rates and therefore increase the cooling effect of the green roof. In addition, Miller says, in some cases it might be impossible or undesirable to connect to a municipal storm sewer system, in which case rainwater and runoff from the green roof and elsewhere on the site can be collected in cisterns and pumped onto the roof for use by plants during drier spells.

Horticulturist and modular system designer David Mac-Kenzie notes that the effort to secure LEED points for water efficiency sometimes keeps irrigation systems out of projects that could benefit from them. Replanting every five or ten years after a drought, he says, is itself not very sustainable. Especially on roofs with a very thin layer of substrate, in areas such as the Pacific Northwest where summers tend to be very dry, or on large projects, an irrigation system can act as a good insurance policy.

Finally, installing an irrigation system makes sense when the client wants to be sure that the green roof will look its best all the time.

Choose the right system

If a source of water is available, a small green roof can be hand-watered with a hose during establishment or drought. Overhead lawn sprinklers can also be used, though they are inefficient. Permanent drip lines and systems with pop-up heads can also be installed and, if desired, automated. Regular checks of such systems should be included in the maintenance specification. Before specifying such a system, make sure it's compatible with your

If an irrigation system is included in the design, make sure it works properly after installation. The emitters on this roof did not sufficiently cover the planted area.

drainage layer: Aggregate will support any system, whereas sheets work with some and not others.

Very sophisticated irrigation systems, using sensors that register soil moisture, are also available. But they might not work properly with green roof medium, which can be too porous for the proper functioning of the sensors. If you or your client is interested in this kind of system, send a sample of your medium blend to the manufacturer to make sure it's compatible with other components (Luckett 2009a).

When he does irrigate his projects, Miller uses flood irrigation at the base of the green roof assembly. A deeper course of medium is needed for this approach, but he says that keeping the upper level of the growing medium dry allows drought-tolerant succulents to thrive while the deeper roots of grasses and perennials can reach down to use the supplemental water. In some dry climates, however, especially during establishment, and with some design effects such as mounded medium, base irrigation might not provide enough plant-available moisture, so supplemental irrigation closer to the surface will still be necessary after installation.

Account for rooftop conditions

Irrigation systems on a green roof are subject to different conditions than those at grade. Exposure to stronger heat and sunlight can degrade materials more quickly, and experience might show that systems for roofs should be made of different materials. Because most green roof assemblies are relatively thin, sprinkler heads might not be adequately covered to avoid damage.

Water pressure is often a problem with rooftop irrigation. Even when there is sufficient pressure when a building is empty, in an office building full of employees or an apartment building full of residents, people will be using other water systems, potentially diminishing pressure significantly. Without enough pressure, the distribution of water can be insufficient to maintain the whole system.

Use resources wisely

Any irrigation system should be designed to operate as efficiently as possible. Green roof irrigation systems can be designed to use harvested rainwater or other nonpotable water. Systems should also operate only when needed. Unnecessary irrigation on a green roof might not hurt the plants, but it can produce a lot of wasteful runoff (Kurtz 2008).

Slope

Green roofs are most common on roofs that are relatively flat. Pitched roofs can be greened, but properly designing a sloped system will require more expertise. Slope also reduces the stormwater retention capacity of a green roof, often dramatically, which is something to keep in mind if stormwater management is a project objective.

Design a stable system

Keeping the elements of the assembly in place and preventing erosion of the growing medium are key objectives when designing green roofs that have a slope beyond a critical point. The rule

The design of sloped green roofs requires stabilization of the components.

A honeycomb-like perforated plastic grid is one way to hold growing medium in place on a slope. Photograph by Cynthia Tanyan

of thumb is that 2:12 (a rise of 2 inches [5 cm] over a run of 12 inches [30 cm]) is the critical pitch (Miller 2009b; NRCA 2009). Achieving this requires a sophisticated understanding of all system interfaces, including those below the medium, where slippage is most likely to occur. The bonding strength of adhesives between layers, including the one attaching the membrane to the deck, cannot be relied upon to stabilize the slope (Miller 2009b).

A green roof assembly on a slope can be held in place by physical supports or retainers along the ridge at the top of the slope, at the eaves at the bottom of the slope, or at intervals along the roof deck. This last approach, known as field support, must be used for very long slopes (Miller 2009b). Growing medium on sloped surfaces is often held in place by a perforated plastic grid or similar structure or by cleats or battens. All of these supports must be carefully installed to avoid damaging the waterproofing membrane.

Understand the impact of slope on drainage

Modular systems and mats can also be used on a slope, but specifying these prevegetated systems should not be a substitute for analysis of the impact the slope will have on the system. With water running off the roof more quickly, the design should account for this drying effect.

Especially on a large pitched roof, the amount of water moving down a slope can potentially overwhelm the system's ability to drain. Because green roofs are a new technology for many designers and engineers, large and complicated projects should be thoroughly vetted by the green roof design team. Don't assume that others on the project thoroughly understand how a green roof system works.

The new headquarters for the Haworth office furniture company in Holland, Michigan, is stunning, with a large green roof that slopes down six stories to grade. This steep slope, the roof's size (45,000 square feet; 4185 square meters), and the fact that the slope narrows as it descends made drainage on this project a particular challenge.

Not all aspects of the challenge were apparent before construction. When the manufacturer of the edging expressed con-

This green roof, at the headquarters of the Haworth furniture company in Holland, Michigan, presented the designers with a drainage challenge.

Perforated metal edging at the base of the slope releases stormwater moving through the system.

cern about the hydraulic pressure that would be generated on the roof during a big storm, modular system designer David MacKenzie realized his company's modules might also lack the capacity to accommodate such pressure. Working with the general contractor and engineers on the project, MacKenzie researched rainfall patterns in the area and investigated design solutions.

He came to believe that elevating the modules would sufficiently ease the movement of water off the roof, and running tests on a similarly pitched mockup roof confirmed this. Manufacturing the specially designed elevated modules added about $0.50 per square foot to the cost of the assembly, says MacKenzie, but it saved on the material and labor costs associated with installing drain boards over the large surface area, another potential solution. Similar experimentation revealed a way to move water along the long base edge of the roof to drain inlets quickly enough to avoid excessive buildup of hydraulic pressure. Perforated edging holds the modular system back 2 feet (0.6 m) from the edge, where a system of drains, covered by pavers, quickly carries extra water away. The perforated edging was also installed along the lower edge of the system, where it meets grade. MacKenzie insisted on drilling extra holes in the edging to make sure water does not build up behind it.

The Haworth roof, which was installed in 2007, has already endured several large storms, including a couple of extreme events with more than 6 inches (15 cm) of rain. Had the installer not recognized the urgency of the drainage challenge, the roof could have failed, causing damage to the building or injury to its inhabitants, but instead it has performed perfectly.

Choose appropriate plants

Slope exacerbates the already harsh hot, dry, and exposed rooftop environment. When specifying plants for a sloped roof, make

A complicated roof will have a lot of microclimates. Plants can struggle in more exposed areas.

sure the species you choose can withstand such conditions. Complex roofs with both flat and sloped surfaces will have microclimates with greater and lesser exposure. More exposed areas will require tougher plants and, if there is an irrigation system, more water than other areas. Protected areas can be good spots to use more delicate species.

Scale

Maximizing most of the nonaesthetic benefits of green roofs, such as mitigation of the urban heat island effect and the reduction of stormwater runoff in densely built cities, requires greening of a lot of roof area. Planting large roofs is a good way to start this process.

Larger green roofs present some challenges, such as wind uplift at corners, especially on taller buildings. But in some respects a huge green roof is easier to design than a small one.

The planting palette for this very large green roof in Culpeper, Virginia, was strategically chosen to produce a self-sustaining landscape.

On a simple extensive project, economies of scale can lower the price per square foot. When stormwater management is an objective, anecdotal evidence from the field indicates that the longer drainage path over a larger surface area promotes much better performance.

Establishing and maintaining a very large roof can be a challenge. Prevegetated methods such as mats and modules can considerably reduce the labor and resources needed. On the Haworth headquarters roof, for example, pregrown modules made possible a one-man maintenance team (who cares for other parts of the large site as well as the roof), as well instant visual gratification for the owner.

Another way to simplify establishment and maintenance in design is to select plants that will easily adapt and self-seed. On the 228,000 square foot (21,205 square meter) roof of the Library of Congress' National Audio Visual Conservation Center in Culpeper, Virginia, plugs and seeds of succulents, perennials, and meadow grasses were selected to provide a kind of controlled succession. Sedums made up most of the primary planting palette to minimize the amount of exposed medium during establishment. Perennials and grasses, selected for a low-growing habit, drought tolerance, and the production of viable but not windborne seed, established more slowly but eventually began to outcompete the succulents and form a meadow landscape. This seed bank of desirable species left little opportunity for a bank of weed seeds to make its way onto the roof and take over, and the roof did not send its own seeds blowing into the surrounding landscape. A quick-draining medium was laid 6 to 8 inches (15 to 20 cm) deep to support the dry perennials, but not so deep as to support a variety of weeds. Its composition, comprising a single-sieve mineral aggregate and compost, also helped to keep the surface dry, making it even more difficult for weeds to establish.

Wind

Once the root system is fully developed, a green roof assembly has good wind resistance. But especially windy sites require special attention during installation and establishment. As a general rule, wind pressure increases with elevation (Luckett 2009a).

Wind scour can erode growing medium on sections of a green roof.

It can be especially strong along the roof's perimeter and at corners. Irrigation lines and other components exposed by wind scour can degrade. Check these areas during maintenance visits.

During installation, insulation and drainage boards and fabrics can be difficult to handle safely (NRCA 2009). Biodegradable blankets or nets can help secure newly installed plants during establishment on a project that is built in place. Sites that are consistently windy can be good candidates for prevegetated systems such as mats or modules. If modules are used, make sure they are heavy enough to stay in place.

Even sites that are not usually subject to high winds should

Right: Biodegradable wind blankets can protect plants during establishment.

Below: This windswept site on the waterfront World Trade Center in Boston is home to the first U.S. green roof project to feature pre-vegetated mats. The mats were internally reinforced by a fabric made of tangled nylon fibers, and they were secured with nylon zip ties to a strong geogrid mesh, which was in turn fastened to buried concrete ballasts. Photograph courtesy of Roofscapes

be checked during maintenance visits for wind effects, especially around the perimeter where a "wind vortex" phenomenon can require protective measures (Luckett 2009a). Even on large roofs, the whole surface should be regularly monitored for wind scour, which can expose fabrics and other components to the elements. Wind can also lift up elements that have been exposed in this way, potentially destabilizing part or all of the green roof assembly.

Shade

Plants in shaded areas on a green roof are subject to less desiccation, but owing to the qualities of growing medium they rarely enjoy more moisture. On a low building shaded by tall trees, specify plants that can tolerate dry shade.

Shade from buildings or other structures is different from the dappled shade cast by trees. Parts of the roof that are in shadow in spring might be fully exposed for much of the day during the summer, when the sun is directly overhead. Glass or light-colored surfaces can reflect light that can heat up and stress plants. Careful analysis of the site should be undertaken before plants are specified, and shade studies should focus on the time of year plants will be most active.

Below left: Shade can provide a sheltered microclimate, but growing medium will remain quite dry.
Photograph by Linda McIntyre

Below right: Shade cast by buildings requires analysis in design.

Integrated sustainable design

Green roofs are most usefully deployed with other natural systems across a whole site design. In most climates, a green roof alone will not keep all rainfall on a site. But, in combination with at-grade measures such as porous pavements or bioretention swales, as part of a sustainable design approach green roofs can make a building site self-mitigating for stormwater runoff

Water that runs off the building's green roof, as well as runoff from the parking lot, flows to this rain garden. All stormwater stays on site.

When solar arrays are used on a green roof, it's important to make sure the membrane is fully protected by the green roof assembly.

(Gangnes 2007). Bioretention areas can also manage any nutrients that leach off the assembly early in its life. Even when more conventional measures such as detention basins are used, green roofs can keep secondary systems smaller and more affordable. As with any other green roof, green roofs used in conjunction with other technologies should be designed and installed in a manner protective of other roofing components, especially the waterproofing membrane.

Contrary to popular belief, green
roofs require regular maintenance
to stay in top form.

5 Maintaining Your Green Roof

Key Points

The best management practices for green roof maintenance are:

- Raise the issue of maintenance early in the design process to underscore its importance.
- If a prevegetated installation method is not used, good plant establishment during the first year or two dramatically reduces the effort required for long-term maintenance on most extensive roofs. Build plant establishment into the program.
- The maintenance team should be prepared to make the appropriate assessments and understand that green roofs require a different approach than landscapes at grade.
- Maintenance visits should be scheduled to be preventative rather that reactive; this requires a basic understanding of plant physiology and weed life cycles.
- Plant and soil health should be monitored and kept in balance.
- Regular roof issues are part of green roof maintenance. The green roof team should make sure waterproofing and other components are intact and functioning well.

While green roofs are sometimes sold to clients as low- or no-maintenance landscapes, this is not a realistic approach to any system comprising living organisms. Nor is doing nothing and hoping for the best a realistic approach to keeping a crucial part of the building envelope functioning in top form.

Regular maintenance is in the interest of everyone involved in a green roof project. It's the key to fulfilling the designer's intent, maximizing the ecosystem services provided by the roof, and protecting the owner's investment. A green roof can be designed for low maintenance, but rarely for zero maintenance. In many cases, failing to maintain a green roof will mask problems that eventually bring about unintended consequences, possibly including the death of most or all desired plants. It might also void applicable warranties. In addition to promoting healthy plants, a program of regular maintenance will extend the life of the roofing components, reduce the frequency and severity of leaks, and reduce ownership costs (Evans 2006).

Green roof maintenance basics

Not too much work is required to maintain most extensive green roofs if the system was properly designed and installed. Nor are the tasks very difficult if performed regularly and the person doing them knows what to look for. Regular, properly timed maintenance is far less difficult and time-consuming than remediation of entrenched problems. Even when mistakes in the design or installation processes, such as poorly specified growing medium, make it difficult for the plants to establish, skilled and attentive maintenance can save the project, especially if tough plants are used.

Make it part of the design process

The time to think and talk about maintenance and the costs of providing it is very early in the design process. Glossing over its importance is unfair to the client. Only upon consideration of the true costs associated with a green roof can an owner make an informed decision on whether it's an appropriate feature for the project.

The resources that a client is willing and able to devote to maintenance should inform the design of the green roof, including the depth and complexity of the system, whether to include irrigation, the plant palette, the planting design, and the method of planting. An articulated or geometric planting design, such as defined stripes or swirls of different plant species, will require a

Roofs that are regularly viewed and that have a deliberate planting design will need maintenance to keep the design intact.

lot of time, effort, and money to maintain. A roof planted with hardy succulents in random patterns will require much less. If a particular distribution of plant species is integral to the roof's design, such as taller plants in one area and shorter species in another, then maintenance might also involve managing the growth of more aggressive desired plants. An inaccessible roof that is not regularly viewed can be maintained to a different aesthetic standard than an amenity roof, even if the amenity is only visual. A client's reluctance or inability to provide or pay for maintenance should automatically take an unusual or ambitious design paradigm off the table, and it might mean that a green roof ought not to be part of the project at all.

Focus on establishment, but look to the long term

Maintenance requirements for most extensive roofs will be most urgent during the first year after installation, as the design is tested against site conditions and plants adapt to the site and grow to fill in open areas. Making sure that plants establish as quickly as possible and keeping down weeds will set the stage for good performance over the longer term. But, as with any roof, regular inspections and routine maintenance undertaken regularly can extend a green roof's life and save money in the long run by deferring much more expensive major remediation or full replacement (Evans 2006). For more details on establishment, see "Provide for long-term performance and success" in chapter 4.

The life of a green roof can be roughly divided into two or three phases: the establishment period; stability, when the system matures and becomes relatively self-sustaining; and perhaps longevity, as the assembly begins to realize its promise of extending the life of the membrane and providing long-term ecosystem services. This last phase is theoretical at this point for extensive green roofs in North America, but steering the system toward this goal is what maintenance is all about.

Find the right maintenance team

Choosing the right team to maintain the roof is likely to prevent problems or nip them in the bud. Often the installer will provide a year or two of maintenance as part of the contract. Good installers learn from maintenance and usually prefer to provide it over the long term. Some also offer maintenance services for roofs they did not install, and this can be a good place to start if you are looking for a provider.

At the end of the installation contract, the client for ongoing maintenance will usually be the building owner or manager. While the owner or manager might (unwisely) choose not to continue a maintenance program over the long term, in any case, at the termination of the original contract, the owner should be in possession of all relevant information about the roof including the specifications of the system components, the plant list, a

planting plan if applicable, and reports from previous maintenance visits.

Philadelphia-based Roofscapes' approach is a good illustration of how this works in practice. "What we currently give clients is a maintenance program description and a maintenance
report," says president Charlie Miller. "The report has a drawing
of the roof, including where all of the plants are supposed to be,
and a plant list with a checkoff for plants present, flowering,
healthy, stressed, and so forth. [Clients] can send us a photo of
weeds or problems. They are supposed to take a soil sample in the
autumn and consult us about fertilizing in the spring." Roofscapes does not require clients to hire a contractor from their network to perform long-term maintenance, but a failure to send
maintenance reports back to the company will void its warranty.

Roofscapes is also working on a database to enable clients to
review their roof's maintenance history and status, plant list, and
other details online. "You can see all of the maintenance reports,
the energy and time that's been invested in your project, and see
pictures of what you have," says Miller. "This is something people
should be interested in, that they should be proud of, and putting a minimum amount of maintenance and care into it is worth
doing." Information organized and stored like this can also be
a valuable resource if the building is sold to a new owner or if a
new team takes over maintenance.

As with design and installation, experience is the best guide
for choosing an effective provider. The person or people doing
the maintenance have to understand what they are seeing. Green
roof maintenance is best done by an individual or crew with
experience working with green roofs and common green roof
weeds and plants, not just landscapes at grade. If you are turn-
ing over green roof maintenance to an in-house staff, see if green
roof–specific training is available from your installer or other
local providers.

Some maintenance companies use a checklist setting out
specific tasks. But if those tasks are described in vague terms—
for example, "check plants" or "check growing medium"—then a
team using this approach could miss important data about the
roof's health and performance by focusing on actions rather than
the health of the roof as a whole system. A team that cannot reli-

ably identify weeds can allow an infestation to spread rapidly, siphoning water and nutrients from desirable plants and potentially damaging essential roof components such as the waterproofing membrane.

Ideally, maintenance visits should be used as opportunities for observation. What is the roof telling you? Are some spots bare while others are lush with greenery? If green, are the green roof plants thriving or have weeds taken over? Where are the microclimates? A checklist does not lend itself to this holistic approach, and a team that lacks the skills to process this kind of information early in the roof's life can allow problems to fester and worsen. Simply checking off boxes on a list risks allowing those problems to escape notice, and they may be relatively easy and straightforward to fix if tackled right away.

Weeds: the first order of maintenance business

Good green roof maintenance consists of assessing, in turn and as a whole, each of the elements of the system. But on most projects, the first order of maintenance business will be dealing with an element that is not, or should not be, part of the system: weeds.

If weeds get a foothold while large areas of medium are exposed, they can be very difficult to eradicate.

For the first year or two after installation of a system built in place, before the desired plants have grown to fill in bare spots in the growing medium, the dominant task in green roof maintenance is usually weeding. While some owners are relaxed about weeds on a green roof, especially if they are relatively attractive, weeds compete with desired plants for nutrients, water, sunlight, and other resources (Allaby 2006). Their roots can also damage roof components such as the waterproofing membrane (Luckett 2009a).

Although a lot of valuable green roof lore has come from Europe, green roofs in North America face different conditions with respect to weeds. A maintenance regime that works in, say, Germany will not be adequate in many regions here, such as the mid-Atlantic, where more rainfall and warmer soil temperatures during the growing season make for more significant and aggressive weed pressure. So designers and builders in North America should plan for maintenance accordingly and not be lulled into complacency by European examples that are unmaintained or need only annual mowing.

Design against weeds

Prevegetated solutions such as pregrown (not just preplanted) modules or mats will require less weeding and in some cases almost none. If manpower for maintenance is scarce, roof access will be difficult, or weed pressure is expected to be unusually high on a site, designers should consider this kind of approach early on. Otherwise, a maintenance program with an emphasis on weed control in the first months and years should be developed early in the design process, and clear responsibility for carrying it out should be assigned in the construction documentation.

The design of a built-in-place green roof can also affect weed pressure. A thin system designed to support a few tough varieties of hardy succulents is unlikely to support a lot of weeds, especially as the desired plants establish cover. A deeper system with a higher organic content in the growing medium, designed to support a wider variety of herbaceous plants and grasses, will provide a more favorable environment for weeds as well. Plugs or cuttings installed more densely will grow in and keep down

Because pregrown modules move the establishment phase off site, after installation little weeding should be required. These modules do not have exposed plastic edges, so they also provide a monolithic appearance.

On a built-in-place roof, a very thin and austere system will support few weeds, and the ones that do start growing will die.
Photograph by Linda McIntyre

weeds more quickly. If the client's commitment to maintenance is limited or in question, reducing weed pressure through design is a good approach.

Deny them entry

Weed seeds can get on a roof in myriad ways. They can come in with the growing medium (see "Be picky about your supplier" in

Take care not to spread weed seeds while trying to eradicate weeds. On this project, the medium was contaminated with weed seeds. When the mature weeds were pulled, the seed-bearing plants were left on the exposed medium, setting the stage for the cycle to begin again.

chapter 2 for suggestions on vetting suppliers and avoiding this situation). They can contaminate good medium that has not been stored properly during construction. They can blow in with the wind, fly in with birds, or walk in on the shoes, clothing, and tools of people installing or maintaining the roof. Tools and shoes should be rinsed before the maintenance team goes on the roof to avoid spreading seeds picked up at grade.

The process of weeding can itself spread weed seeds. To avoid this, start work at the section of the roof with the fewest weeds, saving the worst areas for last. If the weeds have set ripe seed, hold a trash bag or other closed container as close as possible while pulling the weeds. Never use a perforated container, such as a nursery flat tray, to collect weeds.

Know what you're looking for

The identification and removal of weeds is crucial to good maintenance. Hiring a team capable of doing these tasks well and completely will cost more, but a team with no green roof training might not be able to prevent or solve problems, reducing the value of the maintenance visit. Less expertise means opportunities to fine-tune the design can also be lost. Weeds can reveal microclimates—moisture-tolerant weeds such as horsetail (*Conyza ca-*

nadensis), for example, can help reveal the distribution of water on a roof. Wetter areas might simply be cooler and more shaded, or the moisture might indicate a drainage problem. A knowledgeable team can best assess such a situation. The responsible individual or crew, if not well trained in horticulture, should at least have an illustrated list of plants that are supposed to be on the roof, as well as an illustrated list of weeds common to the region (see "Resources" for some recommended weed guides).

Site conditions will also have an impact on weed pressure and the species needing control. Are there trees such as maples hanging over the roof that will produce a lot of seedlings? Is there a grassy meadow nearby that will send a lot of airborne seeds onto the roof? Are there vacant lots infested with invasive species? Is the site configured so that a maintenance crew is likely to bring seeds of spurge or clover up on their shoes? Information from a thorough site analysis will enhance a maintenance program and prepare the team for some of what they are likely to confront on visits. On a large site, good weed control on the at-grade sections of the property can reduce weed pressure on the roof.

As in a garden, on a green roof a weed can be a good plant, even one that is part of the planting design, that's simply in the wrong place. Plants acclimate, grow, and reproduce at different rates, and if the design reflects a balance of species, maintenance

Grasses that are part of the planting design can self-seed aggressively. If the owner wants to maintain the planting design, such plants will have to be kept in check.

will likely be needed to preserve that balance. The maintenance team should have a good understanding of the planting design so that if one plant proliferates to the exclusion of other desired species—this can be a problem with grasses—it can be thinned or otherwise kept in check.

Understand weed life cycles for effective control

Knowing basic information about how weeds grow and set seed will make attempts to control them more effective. The examples described in this section do not comprise an exhaustive list of common green roof weeds; instead they illustrate types of weeds that a maintenance team in any region might encounter.

Annuals

Annual weeds germinate, set seed, and die in a single growing season. Many of them grow rapidly and produce large amounts of seed. Left unchecked, they can cause significant maintenance problems on a green roof.

Euphorbia maculata   spotted spurge
Spurge is a fast-growing annual weed common on green roofs in nearly every climate. Seeds germinate in open soil when it warms

Below left: Euphorbia maculata

Below right: A tiny spurge seedling can produce viable seed in as little as two weeks.

up in late spring. Mature seeds can appear very soon after germination, sometimes within two or three weeks. They become sticky when wet and are therefore dispersed easily, clinging to birds' feet or workers' shoes, tools, or clothes.

CONTROL: This plant loves open areas and is most troublesome on green roofs immediately after installation, before desired plants are well established. Hand-pulling is effective on a small scale. A small propane torch, used with caution, can burn the plants and viable seed. Pre-emergent herbicides can control spurge, but downstream consequences must be considered.

Conyza canadensis syn. *Erigeron canadensis*
  horsetail, mare's tail, horseweed
Horsetail is common in poor soils and vacant lots and is widely distributed throughout North America. It flowers from midsummer to autumn. Seeds germinate soon after ripening, in autumn or in the spring as frost subsides. Summer-germinating seeds will overwinter as rosettes.

CONTROL: Horsetail is easily hand-pulled from green roof medium early in its life cycle.

Galium aparine bedstraw
This plant is widely distributed throughout North America. It

Below left: *Conyza canadensis*

Below right: Rosettes, juvenile forms of horsetail, are easy to pull from coarse green roof medium.

Galium aparine

germinates in early spring and can continue to germinate until early autumn. Bedstraw has a prostrate, vining habit and can climb over desired green roof plants, shading them out.
CONTROL: Hand-pulling is effective if done before the plant is mature. When fully grown, each plant spreads over a large area, making control more difficult and fostering dispersal of seeds.

Perennials

Perennial weeds regrow from their roots after winter dormancy. They do not typically produce the volume of seeds that annual weeds do, but they must be removed completely, including all root material, to avoid regrowth.

Hypochaeris radicata   common or hairy cat's ear, false dandelion
This perennial weed is common west of the Cascade Range. Germinated seeds grow into rosettes, and the mature plant has long stems topped with yellow aster-like flowers.
CONTROL: Weed at the rosette stage, before flowering, making sure to remove the entire root mass.

Taraxacum officinale   dandelion
This perennial weed sprouts from windborne seed and is widely distributed throughout North America. The plant prefers to ger-

Hypochaeris radicata

Above left: *Taraxacum officinale*

Above right: *Trifolium repens*

minate in areas of exposed medium but can also live in proximity to other plants owing to its taproot. It maintains a rosette base throughout the year and can send up flowers any time the climate is favorable. Even a small broken root remnant will form a new rosette.

SIMILAR SPECIES: *Hypochoeris radicata* (common cat's ear), *Hieracium pratense* (hawkweed), *Cichorium intybus* (chicory)

CONTROL: Hand-weeding or spot-spraying before flowering.

Trifolium repens   Dutch clover

Clover, a familiar and widely distributed mat-forming groundcover, is stoloniferous and persistent. It spreads both by seeds and by rooting at the nodes of the stolons.

SIMILAR SPECIES: *Trifolium pratense* (red clover), *Trifolium fragiferum* (strawberry clover), *Trifolium arvense* (rabbitfoot clover), *Lotus corniculatus* (bird's foot trefoil), *Oxalis* (woodsorrel)

CONTROL: Clover is very difficult to remove once established. Strong and expensive measures such as removing desired plants and growing medium or repeated applications of herbicide can be the only solutions if an infestation is not remedied early in the plant's life cycle.

Grasses

Grasses (Gramineae) are one of the most successful plant families in the world, comprising nearly 8000 species. They are widely distributed in every climate and therefore common sources of weed infestations on green roofs. There are both annual and perennial grasses, and each can produce large quantities of seed that remains viable for years.

Setaria glauca   yellow foxtail

This is a very common annual grass species that germinates in summer. Each head can produce 3000 viable seeds.

SIMILAR SPECIES: *Setaria faberi* (giant foxtail), *Setaria viridis* (green foxtail)

CONTROL: Yellow foxtail is very easy to pull early in its life cycle. If allowed to grow, however, green roof medium might come up in the root mass and disturb surrounding plants.

Digitaria sanguinalis   large crabgrass

This is an annual grass with aggressive roots that can grow new plants from root nodes. Crabgrass can grow in almost any soil type and live in very low nutrient environments, making it more difficult to control on a green roof with a dry-down strategy or by mowing.

Setaria glauca

SIMILAR SPECIES: *Digitaria ischaemum* (smooth crabgrass), *Digitaria ciliaris* (southern crabgrass)

CONTROL: As with all grasses, the earlier the plant is removed after germination, the less work to control it over the long run.

Trees

Tree seedlings can pose serious problems for green roofs. They can produce strong root systems that aggressively seek out water

Digitaria sanguinalis

Tree seedlings can damage green roof components and should be removed as soon as possible.

in the seams of the waterproofing membrane, compromising its integrity and potentially causing leaks. The seedlings should be removed as early as possible in their life cycle. Cherries (*Prunus*), mulberries (*Morus*), and other fruits are very popular bird foods, and if such trees are nearby you can expect a lot of their seedlings to appear on the roof. Other species, such as maples (*Acer*) and cottonwoods (*Populus*), have windborne seeds that can also infest nearby sites.

Control established weeds

Some weeds are inevitable in any landscape, including a green roof. Keeping infestations under control does not have to be difficult, expensive, or toxic.

Hand-pulling is best

The best way to eliminate weeds on a green roof is to pull them out by hand. Hand-pulling is usually easily done on a green roof because growing medium, comprising larger particles with fewer fine-textured particles to bind the soil together, is less compacted than garden soil, so roots are less tenacious. Weeding should be done at least twice every year—ideally three or four times—and sessions should be timed so that aggressive weeds do not have the opportunity to set seed.

It's usually easy to pull weeds out of green roof medium by hand.

Benign destruction works well

Weeds can be killed by a blowtorch or by organic substances such as horticultural vinegar that cause no ecological harm. The acetic acid in the vinegar solution works by destroying cell membranes and thus desiccating plants, and it has no impact on soil. It can, however, irritate human skin and cause severe eye damage. Household vinegar, typically a solution of 5 percent acetic acid, is much less effective than commercial preparations with concentrations of up to 20 percent (Webber et al. 2005).

Use chemical controls with caution

When time is an issue or when facing a major weed infestation, it is tempting to resort to common chemical herbicides such as glyphosate. While these products can be effective on green roofs,

Above left: Carefully using a small propane torch to burn weeds and their seeds effectively controls the weeds without harming succulent plants.

Above right: If chemical herbicides must be used, it's best to carefully sponge them onto weed foliage, avoiding the growing medium.

they were designed for use in clay soils. Chemical herbicides can potentially compromise water quality by leaching off the roof in stormwater runoff, owing to the shallowness of the medium and its relative lack of fine particles. At present, no herbicides are labeled for green roof use, although some are labeled for aquatic use. If your roof drains directly into a storm drain, you are essentially managing an aquatic system.

Not enough research has been done to determine the extent to which the use of such chemicals on green roofs poses ecological problems, but it makes sense to exercise caution in the face of so many unknowns. One way to do so is to make sure, if using these chemicals, to apply them to the plant only. Glyphosate, for example, can be sponged onto leaves to avoid leaching from the medium.

Pre-emergent weed killers such as trifluralin and isoxaben have also been used successfully on green roofs. But these chemicals have not been labeled for any use around water. Again, little research has been done to gauge the impact of stormwater runoff carrying these chemicals on the wider environment, so they should be used with caution and avoided if there is water on the site or if runoff is discharged into bodies of water. Pre-emergent herbicides can also prevent the germination of plants intentionally oversown on a green roof, so the individual or crew charged with weed control should be aware of other aspects of the maintenance program that might be affected by the choice of control methods.

Maintaining plant and soil health

Regular attention to newly installed plants and medium and quick remediation of any problems will help promote a robust and long-lived green roof assembly. Rooftop conditions and the characteristics of green roof medium require a different approach than landscapes at grade.

Keep newly installed plugs secure in the medium and sufficiently moist

Keeping the right plants healthy is as important to maintenance as removing the wrong plants. A broad look at plant health can provide general information about the roof and how the system is faring. On a newly installed roof, plugs can heave above the growing medium or be pulled out by curious birds. Hardy suc-

Below left: Just-planted plugs can heave out or be pulled out by birds. Often simply stepping on them will bring the roots back into contact with the medium.

Below right: Biodegradable netting can help protect newly installed plants during establishment.

culents in this condition are usually still alive and can be replanted. On a small roof, simply stepping on unearthed plugs, inserting them deeper into the growing medium, is often enough to solve this problem. An overlay of jute netting or temporarily placed motion-detecting sprinklers can discourage bird activity.

If the growth of plants seems sluggish after installation, check soil moisture first. It could be the case that water is not carrying available fertility to the roots—the medium has to stay moist so the plug or cutting maintains contact. Water moves quickly down a green roof assembly, especially before the roots of newly installed plants grow and spread.

Add the right species to promote good cover

Good observation skills are critical for effective maintenance. On a more established roof, the crew should check whether some species have migrated to particular areas and try to judge which

The succulent plugs on this roof were oversown with cuttings to provide faster cover. Photograph by Linda McIntyre

conditions the plants might find favorable. Is this area more sheltered from wind or strong afternoon sun? Is the medium deeper here? Planting additional plugs, cuttings, or seeds of species that are thriving on a particular part of the roof or its whole can help promote more complete plant cover, improving the roof's functionality and making future maintenance visits easier as well as improving the roof's appearance. The microclimates can be used to refine the plant palette, or they can be further investigated to make sure, for example, wetter areas are draining properly.

Investigate problem areas

Although different plant species will grow at different rates, and these rates will also be affected by microclimatic conditions, areas of widespread dieback or stunted growth among all species should prompt deeper investigation. These conditions could indicate problems including issues with medium. Is it shallower here or of a different composition? The medium might need evening out or supplementation to support the plants well. Is something about the building's structure—perhaps reflection off mechanical units that increases the temperature of the medium—affecting this section of the roof? Maybe a tougher species

Even when most plants are healthy, areas of dieback can occur.

Roof infrastructure can affect plant health. On this roof, reflection off metal penetrations has stressed plants.

should be planted in these areas, or they should be laid with ballast or pavers rather than planted.

Look for signs of stress, damage, or disease

The maintenance team should note the health and growth rate of the plants, both above the growing medium and at the root level. Within a few weeks of installation, plants should begin adapting to local conditions and start to acclimate. You should begin to see strong and healthy new growth. If you dig down around the perimeter of the plant, you should see new white roots going into the medium.

Too little water during establishment can leave plants wilted and with a shrunken root mass. Pale green or yellow leaves are a sign of chlorosis, a response to iron deficiency. Die-out developing in the center of the plant or insect damage can be indicators of disease—insects will often seek out already-stressed plants. The earlier problems are identified, the less it will probably cost to fix and the greater your chance of success.

The maintenance team should check to see if something in the roof infrastructure might have gone awry. Is an irrigation system not working, or is it adjusted improperly and providing too much water? Are drains clogged with plants, medium, or other debris, leaving the assembly waterlogged? Is the sun reflecting off HVAC equipment or other penetrations and overheating plants? Sometimes the planting design will have to be adjusted to accommodate situations like this.

If the maintenance team does not have a lot of horticultural expertise, they should not simply increase irrigation, add fertilizer, or use pesticides just to see what happens. Green roofs, especially extensive green roofs, suffer more often from overwatering and excess fertilization than the reverse.

Keep fertility in balance

Sometimes plant stress can be prevented with maintenance. Botrytis, for example, is a fungus that thrives on plant debris. When plants in a very fertile environment grow taller than normal, the weight of spent flower stalks can topple stems, trapping air close

When plants are in a high-fertility environment, they can grow tall and flop over, inviting fungus infestations. Removing spent flower and seed heads with a small mower or weed trimmer can help prevent this.

to the surface of the growing medium. Plants usually recover, but the fungus can cause some dieback. Keeping the soil fertility in check and removing dead flower and seed heads can prevent the problem.

On a green roof, the objective is to maintain enough fertility for specified plants, but not so much that a lot of nutrients leach off the roof or an attractive environment for weeds or disease is created. At grade, extra fertility rarely causes much direct harm to plants. But if the maintenance crew is more accustomed to managing turf and perennial beds, it's important that they understand that a green roof has different needs.

Maintain soil integrity

In a perfect world, every green roof would be installed with the right medium for the desired plant palette. If there's a persistent problem with the plants that does not appear to be related to one of the situations described above, the problem could be in the medium. If it was not properly specified or blended, the medium might not provide a favorable environment for plants.

Even with the best efforts, the lack of accepted standards and reliable data can make it difficult to assess what type or composition is best for a particular project, especially if species other than hardy succulents comprise a significant portion of the plant list. A supplier with a track record of successful projects and familiarity with FLL and ASTM guidelines and methods will be more likely to provide the right material for your project. Even so, problems can still arise.

Medium should be checked during maintenance visits to make sure its depth is consistent with the design specification. Wind scour, compression, or the decay of organic material can cause the medium to lose volume, potentially compromising the health of the plants.

During its first growing season, good growing medium has enough organic matter for plants to get started. After that, a light annual application of slow-release fertilizer is usually sufficient. But like soil in a garden, green roof medium should also be tested regularly—ideally, every year. Annual tests can help identify problems early, making it easier to prevent significant damage.

Problems with medium often arise with respect to particle distribution. Medium with too many fine particles can impair filter fabrics and drainage systems, resulting in a persistently wet environment that can kill plants, damage components, and undermine the roof deck's structural integrity. Medium can lose almost all its porosity and dry to a bricklike consistency. Testing can determine whether a medium's particle distribution is appropriate.

Testing will also reveal chemical properties, water and air measurements, and nutrient balance. In the absence of regular testing, dead plants and moss can be indicators of an environment too low in nutrients, while heavy weed pressure can signal that it's too high. Indicators such as these should be followed up with a test from a lab experienced with green roof soils and horticulture.

The results of tests might not be easily interpreted by the maintenance team. If the testing lab does not provide an interpretation of the results, make sure to follow up with someone at the lab or another expert who understands the implications of the test results and can suggest remedial measures.

Maintaining the non-green elements of a green roof

Green roof maintenance goes beyond horticulture. All of the roof's elements must be monitored to ensure they are functioning properly. When they aren't, the integrity of the roof as well as the health of the plants can be jeopardized.

Drains and drainage

Maintaining good drainage on a green roof is extremely important. Too much water on the roof could overtax its structural capacity and cause damage and even collapse. Areas of dieback can indicate poor drainage. Look for pooling of water, inconsistent soil moisture, and moss as other potential indicators. Regularly check surface drains and clear out plant growth or debris that could impair their function. As with other aspects of maintenance, clearly defining tasks such as these will make it easier for the maintenance team to provide the best service.

Don't let plants clog drains.

The extent to which plants should grow between pavers can be a matter of preference and should be addressed in the maintenance contract.

Hardscape

On a roof laid with pavers, the maintenance team should check during maintenance visits to make sure the pavers are intact and stable. Beyond this, maintenance requirements for hardscape on a green roof can be subjective. If weeds are growing between pavers, they should be removed to avoid self-seeding. But ground-cover plants can also grow there. Some clients like this softening effect on the design, while others will want exposed spaces kept clean of any plants. These issues should be spelled out in the maintenance contract.

Irrigation

Most extensive green roofs are not irrigated once plants are established. But if there is an irrigation system, it will have to be

Exposed and kinked irrigation lines are unlikely to function properly. If a green roof has an irrigation system, it should be regularly checked during maintenance visits.

maintained. Built-in irrigation systems should be checked at least twice every year in climates where freezes occur. In the spring, when the system is turned on, the maintenance person or team should verify that it is intact and functioning properly and that any sensors are properly calibrated. In the autumn, lines should be drained to avoid damage by freezing. Automated systems should be checked and adjusted frequently.

If horticultural maintenance is being done separately from the maintenance of the irrigation system, the crew should be made aware of the irrigation system so they know the plants are being (or should be) watered regularly and guard against damaging any of the irrigation system components during other maintenance work. The maintenance crew should check during visits for evidence of leakage and exposed lines that can degrade in sunlight.

HVAC and other systems

A building's heating, cooling, and ventilation systems will often have an impact on nearby plants. Heat, dry forced air, and reflected sunlight can stress desired plants, and extra moisture from condensation can foster weeds. Shade cast by penetrations can provide a protected microclimate or make it difficult for

It can be difficult to maintain tight areas around HVAC equipment, and the shelter and condensation can provide a hospitable environment for weeds. Laying this area with coarse gravel rather than planting it would have made it easier to maintain.

Shade cast by HVAC systems can protect or stress plants. Monitor these areas carefully during maintenance visits.

If tradespeople are working on the roof, it's a good idea to schedule a maintenance visit shortly afterward. Debris or spills can stress or kill plants.

plants to grow. When weeds take hold in these areas, it can be difficult to remove them from such awkward spaces. Sometimes it's easier to lay these areas with coarse gravel to discourage any plants from growing in such spaces. If tradespeople are working on the roof, it's a good idea to schedule a maintenance visit soon afterward to check for damage to plants from heavy foot traffic, equipment, or spills.

When maintenance isn't enough

Regular, well-timed maintenance will usually keep problems from careening out of control. But some situations will require a more comprehensive approach. Appropriate design and maintenance will usually prevent such situations from occurring, but owners of deeply troubled projects do have options.

When the wrong plants were specified and installed

Sometimes the cost and effort of remedial maintenance will exceed the cost of starting over, and starting over might mean letting go of a design detail. When plants are installed in single-

On an exposed site, it can be difficult to maintain a distinct planting design. This roof was planted with several single-species drifts, but only the hardiest species could survive. The owner accepted that the specified design was impossible to maintain on this part of the roof, and the entire area was planted with the species that worked.

species groups, for example, sometimes one species cannot establish and thrive in its appointed space. A swath of a different species might work, but, especially in exposed areas, only a mix of tough species may be needed to provide the necessary cover. While a client might prefer a particular color and design, few will want to pay for constant replanting.

On some projects the system as designed cannot support the specified plants. This can happen when designers accustomed to working at grade fail to account for the conditions plants will be subject to on a roof. In some cases it's possible to work up a design that will support such plants with irrigation and protection. But simply installing an ill-considered assortment of plants on an extensive system and hoping for the best is almost certain to end in failure and the need for remediation.

When you have a serious weed infestation

A field of weeds is not what most owners have in mind when they commission a green roof. Occasionally, however, such a situation is acceptable. An infrequently viewed green roof installed for code compliance or stormwater management might function well enough in a weedy state that the owner will not want to undertake the expense of remediation.

More often, the owner will want (or the contract will require) remediation. Simply replacing dead plants, while not ideal, is fairly easy to do. But if weeds have been allowed to colonize the roof, remediation is more complicated. First the owner, consultant, or maintenance team has to decide whether the effort required to destroy the weed seed bank is greater than the effort required to start over with clean growing medium. If at all possible, killing the weeds will be easier than removing and reinstalling medium if the physical properties of the medium are appropriate.

A dogged and sustained attack on weeds, removing them before they go to seed, might suffice. Hand-pulling is the best approach, though careful spraying might be appropriate until seed bank is used up. Every time a weed is pulled up, more of the growing medium is exposed to the air, providing new germination opportunities, because most weeds germinate in the top

The original plant palette for this roof comprised native herbaceous perennials, but the medium's depth and granular distribution could not support these plants. Almost none of the specified plants lived, but weed seedlings proliferated. A consultant is working with the owner to determine a more appropriate hardy succulent plant palette.

0.25 inch (0.6 cm) of soil. On a large built-in-place green roof without a lot of infrastructure or penetrations, sheets of black plastic can kill the seeds with heat. When weeds stop germinating, replanting can begin.

New medium: the last-ditch alternative

Removal and replacement of the growing medium, while not something to be undertaken lightly, is sometimes the only option to salvage a project. It must be done with care to avoid unnecessarily exposing or damaging other components, including the waterproofing membrane. Even so, it might void the other components' warranties. Owners contemplating this step should check with the membrane manufacturer for warranty information and advice to mitigate damage during the process. They should also check records to see whether the green roof installer provided a removal and replacement warranty.

The roof at Dansko at the height
of bloom.

Sample Specification

This sample specification is provided courtesy of Green Roof Service LLC, Forest Hill, Maryland. It illustrates how the process works for a project similar to the Dansko headquarters discussed in "Green roofs as amenity spaces" in chapter 4.

Part 1. General

1.1. Summary of Work

A. Green Roof System: Provide a complete green roof system as indicated on the concept drawings, including protection fabric, drain conduit, and inspection boxes, granular drainage layer, filter fabric, growing medium, plant materials, drainage stone, and pavers.

B. Mobilization: Provide all labor, materials, logistics, services, and equipment as necessary to supply and execute the project, including temporary traffic barriers and unloading area at street level; a crane, lift, or derrick to lift materials; dumpsters; and permits and approvals required for execution of the project.

1.2. Definitions

A. Separation and Protection Mat: A fabric that separates the root barrier from the green roof system and protects the root barrier from mechanical impact. An additional function is to store water.

B. Retaining Edge: An L-shaped piece of metal separating different materials horizontally. Side walls have to be slotted to avoid water blockage.

C. Drain Box: A box with a lid installed over the roof drain that allows water to flow into the drain but keeps other materials away from it. Lid must be lockable and perforated.

D. Drainage Channel: A triangular-shaped element (cross section) that is embedded in granular drainage media in order to carry excess water to roof drains and scuppers.

E. Drainage Stone: A coarse granular material such as river stone or crushed stone that is heavy to resist uplift and has a high drainage capacity.

F. Drainage Medium: A granular material such as lightweight aggregate that creates sufficient air space for excess water to move to the roof drains and also retains water to promote plant life.

G. Filter Fabric: A material that creates a separation between the soil media and the drainage layer. Fines and organic particles cannot pass through the fabric. Roots are able to grow through.

H. Growing Medium: A growing medium containing lightweight mineral and organic components engineered for extensive green roofs in multi-course construction.

I. Pavers: A material that is used as surface for patios and as a maintenance path.

J. Bedding: A granular material that is used beneath the pavers for leveling and placement.

K. Plugs: Plants cultivated in multi-cell plates. The size of the cells is determined by the number of cells per plate.

1.3. Submittals

A. Product Data: For each type of green roofing product specified, include data substantiating that materials comply with requirements.

B. There is a single source responsibility for all components of the green roof system.

C. Alternative materials can only be accepted if they are proven equivalent to the ones specified in Part 2. Samples, specifications, and test reports of alternative materials have to be submitted with the proposal. Sample sizes required for alternative materials: 12 by 12 inch (30 by 30 cm) square of any fabric; 1 gallon (3.8 L) bag of any granular material; 1 inch (2.5 cm) of retaining edge.

1.4. Warranty

A. The Contractor shall supply the owner with a minimum one-year workmanship warranty. It is the responsibility of the green roofing contractor to ensure that the plant life is healthy and thriving and all green roofing components are properly functioning for a period of one year.

The Contractor's warranty shall not limit the Contractor's obligation with respect to State or Government laws or statutes.

1.5. Maintenance Program

A. The green roofing Contractor will provide all green roofing maintenance necessary to ensure a healthy green roof system for a period of one year. This shall include, but is not limited to, weeding, feeding, irrigating, replacing plants that die, as required.

Part 2. Products

2.1. Green Roof Material Description

A. Protection Mat: A nonwoven geotextile made from recycled polypropylene that is puncture resistant and has a water storage capacity of 0.10 gallon per square foot (4 L per square meter), making it ideal for protection and supplemental water storage.
    Weight: 15 ounces per square yard (500 g per square meter)
    Product: Optigreen Standard Protection Mat or equivalent
    Supplier: Conservation Technology, 1.800.477.7724 or sales@conservationtechnology.com

B. Retaining Edge: An L-shaped metal board system made from a 60 mil (1.5 mm) tempered aluminum alloy with holes on the vertical leg for water penetration. The edging system includes connectors to avoid gaps between the elements and prefabricated corners.
    Dimension: 6 inches (15 cm) high and wide
    Product: Optigreen Aluminum Edge or equivalent
    Supplier: Conservation Technology, 1.800.477.7724 or sales@conservationtechnology.com

C. Drain Box: A squared inspection box made of UV-protected ABS plastic with lateral water flow holes. Lid as lockable cover with holes for surface water runoff.
    Dimension: 1 square foot (0.09 square meter)
    Height: 4 inches (10 cm)
    Product: Optigreen Drain Box or equivalent
    Supplier: Conservation Technology, 1.800.477.7724 or sales@conservationtechnology.com

D. Drainage Channel: A black ABS plastic drainage element with rows of slots on each side. The unique triangular cross section provides optimal surface area and prevents the channel from floating upward. Triangle Tees are used to join Triangular Drainage Channels in order to make drainage manifolds. The unique interlocking end design permits 90 degree rotation and requires no tools for assembly. Calculate one channel element per every 40 square feet (3.7 square meters) of green roof area and one Tee element for every six channel elements.

Dimension: Channel elements are 40 inches (100 cm) long and 2 inches (5 cm) tall

Product: Optigreen Triangular Drainage Channel or equivalent

Supplier: Conservation Technology, 1.800.477.7724 or sales@conservationtechnology.com

E. Drainage Stone: Crushed stone used in nonvegetated perimeter conditions.
Aggregate type: $3/4$ to 1 inch washed river stone

F. Drainage Medium: A granular drainage material for extensive green roofs in multi-course construction compliant with the German FLL Green Roof Guidelines. The material should be a mixture of all mineral components satisfying the following specifications:

Grain size distribution

retained US $3/8$ (d = 9.50 mm): 0–15 mass percent

retained US #4 (d = 4.75 mm): 70–90 mass percent

retained US #8 (d = 2.36 mm): 93–100 mass percent

retained US #16   (d = 1.18 mm): 95–100 mass percent

proportion of slurry-forming components (d ≤ 0.063 mm): ≤ 10 mass percent

Apparent density (volume weight)

when dry: < 0.70 g/cm^3

at maximum water capacity: < 0.95 g/cm^3

Water and air management

water permeability mod. Kf: ≥ 180 mm/min

pH value, salt content

pH value (in CaCl$_2$): 6.0–8.5

salt content (gypsum extract): ≤ 2.5 g/L

Additional requirements

absence of any phytotoxic substances

fire resistance

frost resistance

Suggested product: Rooflite Drain or equivalent.

Manufacturer: Skyland USA LLC, 1.877.268.0017 or www.skyland.us

G. Separation Fabric: A nonwoven geotextile made from recycled polypropylene that is significantly less likely to clog than common filter fabrics. It is ideal for separating green roof soils from underlying drainage media.

Weight: 6 ounces per square yard (22 g per square meter)

Product: Optigreen Separation Fabric or equivalent

Supplier: Conservation Technology, 1.800.477.7724 or sales@conservationtechnology.com

H. Growing Medium: A green roof growing medium for extensive green roofs in multi-course construction compliant with the German FLL Green Roof Guidelines. The material should be a mixture of mineral and organic components satisfying the following specifications.

Granulometric distribution

passing US #100 (d = 0.15 mm): ≤ 22 mass percent
passing US #50 (d = 0.30 mm): ≤ 32 mass percent
passing US #30 (d = 0.60 mm): ≤ 44 mass percent
passing US #16 (d = 1.18 mm): 12–55 mass percent
passing US #8 (d = 2.36 mm): 35–75 mass percent
passing US #4 (d = 4.75 mm): 53–95 mass percent
passing US 3/8 (d = 9.50 mm): 80–100 mass percent
proportion of slurry-forming components (d ≤ 0.063 mm): ≤ 15 mass percent

Apparent density (volume weight)

when dry: < 0.85 g/cm^3
at maximum water capacity: < 1.35 g/cm^3

Water and air measurements

total pore volume: ≥ 65 volume percent
maximum water holding capacity: ≥ 35 volume percent
air-filled porosity at maximum water capacity: ≥ 10 volume percent
water permeability (saturated hydraulic conductivity): ≥ 0.024 in/min

pH value, salt content

pH value (in CaCl$_2$): 6.5–8.5
salt content (water extract): ≤ 3.5 g/L
salt content (gypsum extract): ≤ 2.5 g/L

Organic substances

organic content: 65 g/L

Additional requirements

absence of any phytotoxic substances
absence of seeds capable of germination
absence of plant parts capable of germination
absence of foreign substances
fire resistance
frost resistance

Suggested Product: Rooflite Extensive MC or equivalent
Manufacturer: Skyland USA LLC, 1.877.268.0017 or www.skyland.us
Alternative products require the submission of an FLL test certificate and a material sample.

I. Pavers: Concrete pavers for patios and maintenance path

Dimensions: 2 feet × 2 feet × 2 inches
Color: gray

J. Bedding: Bedding material should consist of frost-resistant lightweight aggregate like expanded shale or expanded clay. Particle size: 3/16 to 1/4 inch. Note: Granular drainage as specified above can also be used as bedding material.

K. Plugs

Sedum 'Immergrünchen': 72 cell plug
Sedum album 'Murale': 72 cell plug
Sedum album 'Coral Carpet': 72 cell plug
Sedum rupestre 'Angelina': 72 cell plug
Sedum kamtschaticum: 72 cell plug
Sedum kamtschaticum var. *floriferum* 'Weihenstephaner Gold': 72 cell plug
Sedum reflexum: 72 cell plug
Sedum sexangulare: 72 cell plug
Sedum spurium 'Fuldaglut': 72 cell plug
Sedum spurium 'Roseum': 72 cell plug
Sedum spurium 'White Form': 72 cell plug
Talinum calycinum: 72 cell plug
Suggested plant supplier: Emory Knoll Farms, 410.452.5880 or www.greenroofplants.com

Part 3. Execution

3.1. General

A. All components are to be installed by a single Contractor. The various layers shall be installed in such manner as to not puncture any previously installed component.

3.2. Inspection

A. Prior to submitting a bid, and again prior to beginning work, the Contractor shall visit the site to become familiar with the existing conditions.

B. Protecting the waterproofing membrane has to be first priority and any suspected or visible impact of the waterproofing membrane shall be reported to the project manager immediately.

3.3. Roof Protection

A. Arrange work sequence to avoid use of newly constructed roof deck for storage, walking surface, and equipment. Where such access is absolutely required, the Contractor shall provide all necessary protection and barriers to segregate the work area and to prevent damage to adjacent areas. Both plywood and polyester felt protection should be provided for all roof areas that receive traffic during construction.

B. Prior to and during installation, all dirt, debris, and waste material shall be removed promptly.

C. The Contractor shall follow all safety regulations as recommended by OSHA.

D. If any damage occurs to the underlying roofing membrane system and water is allowed to enter the structure under the completed roofing, the affected area shall be removed and replaced at the Contractor's expense.

3.4. Delivery, Storage, and Handling

A. Deliver materials in original, unopened packaging.

B. Ship all materials and plants just in time to minimize on-site storage.

C. Store materials so that the structural capacity of the roof deck is not exceeded.

D. Store the materials within the environmental conditions recommended by the manufacturer.

E. Remove damaged materials from the site promptly and replace with new materials.

3.5. Installation of Green Roof System

A. Separation Fabric: Install separation and protection fabric on top of the complete waterproofing system. Overlap seams at least 4 inches (10 cm) and tack seams using a hot-air welding gun or water the fabric to hold the fabric in place. Parapets, walls, and any technical feature penetrating the waterproofing membrane shall be covered up at 4 inches (10 cm) high from the horizontal surface of the roof membrane. Cut holes into the fabric at all roof drains matching the drain size. Use scissors instead of knives for any cutting of the fabric.

B. Retaining Edge: Place retaining edge on top of the separation and protection fabric. Install connectors between all elements and align all sides carefully according to layout plan. Use prefabricated corner pieces for all 90 degree and 270 degree corners.

C. Drain Boxes: Assemble and install drain boxes over all roof drains according to supplier's recommendations. Place drain boxes on top of the protection fabric.

D. Drainage Channel: For optimum performance, every point of the roof should be within two channel lengths of a drain channel. Layout patterns should be according to supplier's recommendations.

E. Drainage Stone: Place the drainage stone in all areas indicated in the green roof design plan on top of the protection fabric. Dispense and place stone material carefully to avoid damage of roof structure and waterproofing membrane. Level the drainage stone to the thickness of 2 inches (5 cm). Drainage stone strips shall be 18 inches (45 cm) wide.

F. Drainage Medium: The granular drainage material shall be dispensed on the roof in a manner that will not suddenly increase the roof load. The substrate shall immediately be spread and leveled to the designated depth of 2 inches (5 cm).

G. Filter Fabric: Cover drainage medium and drainage stone strips with filter fabric. Use scissors for cutting the fabric and overlap seams at least 4 inches (10 cm). Avoid walking on the filter fabric and the drainage surface as far as possible. Protect often-used areas with plywood or other equivalent materials. Cut off all material covering the drainage stone and trim all edges carefully after the growing medium has been installed and sedum cuttings have been spread.

H. Extensive Soil Layer: Place the growing medium on the filter fabric. The medium shall be dispensed at the roof level in a manner that will not suddenly increase the roof load. Avoid getting any of the growing medium in the overlapping seams of the filter fabric. Minimize walking on the leveled surface of the extensive soil as far as possible. Protect often used areas with plywood or equivalent materials. Level the extensive soil evenly. Consider common compaction rates for this kind of material. Final depth of the growing medium after compaction and consolidation shall be 2 inches (5 cm).

General Instructions for the Placement of Growing Medium: Avoid overburdening structural capacity of roof deck. Avoid sudden impact of heavy loads on the roof. Avoid affecting integrity of underlying layers of green roof system. Keep growing medium from getting under the filter fabric. Keep growing medium from contaminating surrounding areas. Observe specified medium depth. Check depth of already placed medium frequently. Consider compaction. Avoid using installed areas for transportation. Protect areas being used for transportation. Level out surface evenly according to specifications and drawings. Avoid contamination of growing medium. Protect integrity of growing medium.

I. Pavers: Dispense bedding material onto the protection mat and level it out to an even layer of 2 inches (5 cm). Place pavers on the leveled bedding material. The finished surface of the paved area has to be smooth and even, without gaps in between the pavers.

J. Planting: Plants shall be installed two pieces per square foot in random distribution of patches to create meadow effect. Plants shall be set into the growing medium to the full depth of their root system, and growing medium shall be pressed firmly around the installed plant. Avoid walking on planted areas, and eliminate footprints in planted areas. Soak planted areas thoroughly with water.

3.6. Maintenance

A. Irrigation: The goal is to avoid damage due to drought and to get drought-resistant vegetation at the same time. There is no way to predict the exact effort that might be necessary, because local weather conditions have a strong influence. Within the first couple of weeks, periods without considerable rain or irrigation should not be longer than two or three days, depending on the temperature. After two weeks, when plants have started to grow into the medium, periods without rain or irrigation can be slowly extended. After four months, irrigation can be reduced to a minimum. Once plants have fully established, they can tolerate periods of drought lasting several weeks.

B. Weeding: Green roofs are a piece of nature and are built with natural materials. Although material suppliers try to eliminate weed seeds as much as possible, contamination cannot be avoided completely. Some seeds might even be airborne. The primary goal is to avoid that initial weeds get a chance to grow and spread seeds.

   For the first couple of months after installation, the green roof should be checked weekly for weed growth. Pull all weeds by hand and put them in a plastic bag or container to avoid spreading seeds. After the initial phase, weeding should be done at least once a month. Monthly weeding is only necessary from March to October. Chemical weeding is not allowed.

C. Pruning and Trimming: Pruning and trimming as needed to maintain proper appearance and plant health.

D. Plant Replacement: Remove and replace dead plants immediately.

E. Cleaning: Clean all areas of any debris. Keep paved areas and gravel strips free of plant growth. Inspect roof drains regularly, and clean drains if necessary.

F. Duration: Maintenance covered by this contract will end one year after installation.

3.7. Field Quality Control

A. Arrange for Project Manager to inspect green roof installation on completion to provide third party verification of proper installation.

B. Notify Owner 72 hours in advance of inspection.

C. Provide final completion of green roofing in compliance with the specifications and industry standards.

3.8. Completion of Work

A. Prior to the completion of the work it shall be inspected by the Owner and Project Manager. All defects, noncompliance with the specifications, or other recommendations must be corrected immediately by the Contractor prior to completion of the work.

B. All warranties shall be submitted for acceptance prior to final payment.

Resources

A lot of information about green roofs is available online and in print. No list, including this one, will be comprehensive or stay up-to-date for any length of time. But the following are some good resources for learning more about green roofs.

General information about green roof technology and research projects

Colorado State University green roof information is available at http://greenroof.agsci.colostate.edu/

Columbia University's Center for Climate Systems Research Green Roofs site allows visitors to compare data among several instrumented projects (click on links on the right side of the screen for project information and to view data graphs): http://www.ccsr.columbia.edu/cig/greenroofs/

Columbia University's Education Center for Sustainable Engineering is working on ways to accurately measure and improve green roof performance: http://sustainengineering.org/projects/green-roofs/

German Landscape Research, Development, and Construction Society (known by its German initials FLL) provides English-language information, and the guidelines can be purchased at http://www.roofmeadow.com/technical/fll.php

Greenroofs.com is a website that aggregates news articles, industry information, and listings of upcoming conferences and events. It is frequently updated and maintains a large searchable database of projects: http://www.greenroofs.com/

Green Roofs for Healthy Cities, a Toronto-based trade association, holds an annual conference and trade show, administers an awards program, sells training materials, and recently developed an accreditation program. Lists of projects that have won awards and member companies and firms can provide a starting point for identifying potential designers and installers: http://www.greenroofs.org/

The International Green Roof Association holds conferences and disseminates information about green roofs: http://www.igra-world.com/index.php

The Lady Bird Johnson Wildflower Center conducts native plant green roof research: http://www.wildflower.org/greenroof/

Livingroofs.org is a United Kingdom–based website that compiles project information and research; it also includes a link to a do-it-yourself guide for small projects available for purchase: http://www.livingroofs.org/

Michigan State University's Green Roof Research Program website provides general green roof information as well as updates on research projects: http://www.hrt.msu.edu/greenroof/

Oregon State University's green roof research is available at http://hort.oregonstate.edu/greenroof_block

Penn State University's Center for Green Roof Research studies green roof performance, including stormwater quantity and quality, and tests materials: http://web.me.com/rdberghage/Centerforgreenroof/Home.html

Southern Illinois University's Green Roof Environmental Evaluation Network: http://www.green-siue.com/home.html

University of Arkansas' School of Architecture green roof research: http://architecture.uark.edu/500.php

U.S. General Services Administration provides a list of green roofs on U.S. federal government facilities throughout the country, including some project information such as square footage and year of installation: http://www.gsa.gov/Portal/gsa/ep/contentView.do?contentType=GSA_BASIC&contentId=25943&noc=T

Policies and incentives supporting green roof construction

The American Institute of Architects wrote a report that provides a helpful discussion of the advantages and disadvantages of different kinds of local green incentive programs: http://www.aia.org/advocacy/local/incentives/AIAB028722

Greenroofs.com provides information about green roof policies, incentives, and grants on the industry support page: http://www.greenroofs.com/Greenroofs101/industry_support.htm

Paladino and Company prepared a good summary and analysis of various green roof policies and incentive programs for the City of Seattle, which is available on the city's green roof website (scroll down to "Academic" and click on the link for "Sustainable Policies and Incentives Samples"): http://www.ci.seattle.wa.us/dpd/GreenBuilding/OurProgram/Resources/TechnicalBriefs/DPDS_009485.asp

The U.S. Environmental Protection Agency offers a series of documents to help local governments integrate green infrastructure into their policies. Among other issues, the documents, posted as they become available, address funding options and incentives. EPA Municipal Handbook: Managing Wet Weather with Green Infrastructure: http://cfpub2.epa.gov/npdes/greeninfrastructure/munichandbook.cfm

Chicago

Chicago offers a density bonus, grants for green roof construction, expedited permitting, and reduced stormwater fees. Projects that receive public assistance or are subject to review by the city's planning department as a "Planned Development" or "Lakefront Protection Ordinance Development" are usually required to green a percentage of roof area. The city's green roof website offers a guide for building green roofs, a list of providers, information about required permits, and videos about featured projects: http://www.artic.edu/webspaces/greeninitiatives/greenroofs/main.htm

New York

A tax credit for green roof construction, applicable in New York City, was approved by the state legislature and entered into effect in 2009: http://www.nyc.gov/html/dof/html/property/property_tax_reduc_taxreductions.shtml

Philadelphia

Philadelphia's stormwater manual recognizes green roofs as a best management practice. Green roofs designed according to technical standards in the manual are not counted as impervious area, thereby lowering stormwater fees. The text of the manual, including design requirements for green roofs, is available at http://www.phillyriverinfo.org/programs/SubProgramMain.aspx?Id=StormwaterManual

The city offers a credit toward the business privilege tax for 25 percent of the cost of green roof installation (up to $100,000) for roofs that comprise 50 percent of total roof area or 75 percent of eligible roof area, whichever is greater. Tax credit legislation is available at www.phila.gov/revenue/pdfs/Internet_Summary_-_B.pdf

Portland, Oregon

Portland offers grants, a density bonus, and a reduction in stormwater fees for green roofs. Most new city-owned buildings are required to have at least 70 percent green roof coverage. The city's Bureau of Environmental Services Ecoroof information site includes information on codes, incentives, and grants; fact sheets; case studies; performance data; research links; and an Ecoroof Handbook in pdf format: http://www.portlandonline.com/bes/index.cfm?c=44422

Seattle

In Seattle, green roofs qualify as an acceptable strategy for reducing impervious area under stormwater flow control requirements. Green roofs can also be used to help meet the Green Factor requirements for planted coverage in some commercial areas. The city has a helpful website with both basic information and links to (among other things) local codes and incentives, monitoring studies, green roof projects in the area, case studies, and other cities' green roof websites. The city's Department of Planning and Development is developing technical guidelines for green roof construction and is using local data to inform an updated hydrologic model to more precisely quantify the stormwater performance of green roofs: http://www.seattle.gov/dpd/GreenBuilding/OurProgram/Resources/TechnicalBriefs/DPDS_009485.asp

Toronto

In 2009 Toronto became the first city in North America to require green roofs on most large new construction projects. The law takes effect in 2010 for residential, commercial, and institutional projects and in 2011 for industrial projects. Details are available at http://www.toronto.ca/greenroofs/index.htm

Washington, D.C.

The district's Department of the Environment has established a pilot program that offers a subsidy of $5 per square foot, up to $20,000 per project, for eligible green roof construction. At least 50 percent of roof space (excluding utility infrastructure and skylights) must be vegetated, and the course of growing medium must be at least 3 inches (7.5 cm) deep. Details are available at http://ddoe.dc.gov/ddoe/cwp/view,a,1209,q,499460.asp

Professional and industry information

Local chapters of professional associations can help identify experienced green roof designers and installers.

American Institute of Architects (AIA): http://www.aia.org/index.htm; AIA sustainability resources for clients: http://www.aia.org/practicing/groups/kc/AIAS077433; AIA Committee on the Environment Top Ten Green Projects 1997–present: http://www.aiatopten.org/hpb/; AIA 50 strategies toward a 50 percent reduction in building use of fossil fuels (includes sections on green roofs and related issues such as life cycle assessment): http://www.aia.org/practicing/groups/kc/AIAS077430

American Society of Landscape Architects (ASLA): http://www.asla.org/; ASLA Green Roof Project: http://land.asla.org/050205/greenroofcentral.html; ASLA Green Infrastructure Guide: http://www.asla.org/ContentDetail.aspx?id=24076

Construction Specifications Institute and Construction Specifications Canada. The Recommended Format for Construction Specifications is available at http://www.csinet.org/s_csi/sec.asp?TRACKID=&CID=1352&DID=11123

Factory Mutual Global: http://www.fmglobal.com/. Factory Mutual Global Data Sheets, including Property Loss Prevention Data Sheet 1-35: Green Roof Systems, can be downloaded free of charge at http://www.fmglobaldatasheets.com

National Roofing Contractors' Association: http://www.nrca.net/. The association publishes a manual for green roofs, including helpful design details. It can be purchased at http://www.nrca.net/rp/pubstore/details.aspx?id=514/. NRCA's Center for Environmental Innovation in Roofing publishes some information about green roofs: http://www.roofingcenter.org/main/home

Building certification programs

The Green Globes assessment and rating system was developed in Canada and originally based on the United Kingdom's Building Research Establishment's Environmental Assessment Method. It is also used in the United States. Learn more at http://www.greenglobes.com/

The Leadership in Energy and Environmental Design (LEED) program was developed by the U.S. Green Building Council. Join the group or find general information about green building at http://www.usgbc.org/

The U.S. government's Energy Star program, well known for its appliance ratings, can also certify commercial buildings and manufacturing plants. Learn more at http://www.energystar.gov/index.cfm?c=business.bus_bldgs

Accreditation programs

The Green Building Certification Institute was established in January 2008 to run the U.S. Green Building Council's LEED accreditation program. It has since taken over the certification of LEED buildings as well: http://www.gbci.org/

Green Roofs for Healthy Cities, an industry trade association based in Toronto, recently established a Green Roof Professional accreditation program: http://greenroofs.org/index. php?option=com_content&task=view&id=170&Itemid=86

References useful for green roof maintenance

Much of green roof maintenance involves identifying and removing weeds. The following are some helpful guides.

The Canadian government maintains an online weed information and identification resource available at http://www.weedinfo. ca/home.php

Common Weed Seedlings of the North Central States by Andrew J. Chomas, James J. Kells, and J. Boyd Carey. 2001. Available in pdf form at *fieldcrop.msu.edu/documents/Ncr607.pdf*

Field Guide to Noxious and Other Selected Weeds of British Columbia by Roy Cranston, David Ralph, and Brian Wikeem. 2002. Available online at http://www.agf.gov.bc.ca/cropprot/ weedguid/weedguid.htm

An IPM Pocket Guide to Weed Identification in Nurseries and Landscapes by Steven A. Gower and Robert J. Richardson. 2007. Available from Michigan State University Extension at http:// www.ipm.msu.edu/weeds-nursery/contents.htm

Northwest Weeds by Ronald J. Taylor. 1990. Missoula, Montana: Mountain Press.

U.S. Department of Agriculture's Plants Database (http://plants. usda.gov/java/noxiousDriver) contains federal and state lists of noxious weeds and invasive plants, as well as information, including photographs, about weeds by botanical and common names.

Weeds of the North Central States. 1981. North Central Regional Research Publication No. 281, Bulletin 772. Urbana-Champaign: University of Illinois.

Weeds of the Northeast by Richard H. Uva, Joseph C. Neal, and Joseph M. Ditomaso. 1997. Ithaca, New York: Cornell University Press.

Weeds of the South by Charles T. Bryson, Michael S. DeFelice, and Arlyn Evans. 2009. Athens: University of Georgia Press.

Weeds of the West by Larry C. Burrill, Steven A. Dewey, David W. Cudney, B. E. Nelson, and Tom D. Whitson. 1996. Las Cruces, New Mexico: Western Society of Weed Science.

Other green roof books

Planting Green Roofs and Living Walls by Nigel Dunnett and Noel Kingsbury. 2008. Portland, Oregon: Timber Press. This book has a wealth of information and imagery, mostly about European green roofs.

Roof Gardens: History, Design, Construction by Theodore Osmondson. 1999. New York: W. W. Norton. If you want information on intensive green roofs, this is a good place to start.

Selected Bibliography

Allaby, M., ed. 2006. *Oxford Dictionary of Plant Sciences*. Oxford University Press, New York.

Almeda, F. No date. Video describing the plant selection process for the California Academy of Sciences green roof. Available at http://www.calacademy.org/academy/building/the_living_roof/.

American Horticultural Society (AHS). Plant Heat-Zone Map. Available at http://www.ahs.org/pdfs/05_heat_map.pdf.

American Institute of Architects (AIA). 2008. Local Leaders in Sustainability: Green Incentives. Available at http://www.aia.org/advocacy/local/incentives/AIAB028722.

ASTM International. 2007. Sustainability Subcommittee Launches Development of Proposed Green Roof Guide. *Standardization News* July. Available at http://www.astm.org/SNEWS/JULY_2007/roof_jul07.html.

ASTM International. 2009. Annual Book of ASTM Standards. Volume 04.12 Building Constructions (II): E1671–latest; Sustainability; Property Management Systems; Technology and Underground Utilities. E2396: Standard Testing Method for Saturated Water Permeability of Granular Drainage Media [Falling-Head Method] for Green Roof Systems. E2397: Standard Practice for Determination of Dead Loads and Live Loads Associated with Green Roof Systems. E2398: Standard Test Method for Water Capture and Media Retention of Geocomposite Drain Layers for Green Roof Systems. E2399: Standard Test Method for Maximum Media Density for Dead Load Analysis (includes tests to measure moisture retention potential and saturated water permeability of media). E2400: Standard Guide for Selection, Installation, and Maintenance of Plants for Green Roof Systems.

Autodesk/AIA Green Index Survey. 2008. Available at http://images.autodesk.com/adsk/files/2008_autodesk-aia_green_index_report_final.pdf.

Bass, B. 2007. Green Roofs and Green Walls: Potential Energy Savings in the Winter. Report on Phase I. Adaptation and Impacts Research Division, Environment Canada at the University of Toronto Centre for Environment. Available at *www.upea.com/pdf/greenroofs.pdf*.

Bauers, S. 2009. Breaking Ground with a $1.6 Billion Plan to Tame Water. *Philadelphia Inquirer* 27 September. Available at http://www.philly.com/inquirer/front_page/20090927_Breaking_ground_with_a__1_6_billion_plan_to_tame_water.html.

Beattie, D., and R. Berghage. 2004. Green Roof Media Characteristics: The Basics. In Greening Rooftops for Sustainable Communities, Proceedings of the Second North American Green Roofs Conference, Portland, Oregon, June. Available at http://guest.cvent.com/EVENTS/Info/Summary.aspx?e=65ca54a3-0023-419c-949b-d2382747e4cb.

Bingham, L. 2009. Far from Tar: Ecoroofs Take Root in Portland. *The Oregonian*; reprinted in 20 January 2009 edition of *The Daily News*. Available at http://www.tdn.com/articles/2009/01/21/this_day/doc49750e7030e38508362102.txt.

Booth, D., B. Visitacion, and A. C. Steinemann. 2006. Damages and Costs of Stormwater Runoff in the Puget Sound Region. Available at http://www.psparchives.com/our_work/stormwater.htm.

Borden, K., and S. Cutter. 2008. Spatial Patterns of Natural Hazards Mortality in the United States. *International Journal of Health Geographics* 7:64

Brenneisen, S. 2003. The Benefits of Biodiversity from Green Roofs: Key Design Consequences. Prepared for the Greening Rooftops for Sustainable Communities conference, Chicago. Available at http://guest.cvent.com/EVENTS/Info/Summary.aspx?e=65ca54a3-0023-419c-949b-d2382747e4cb.

Brenneisen, S. 2006. Space for Urban Wildlife: Designing Green Roofs as Habitats in Switzerland. *Urban Habitats* 4. Available at http://www.urbanhabitats.org/v04n01/wildlife_full.html.

Buckley, B. 2009. Eco-Design Risks: The Gray in Green: As Sustainable Design and Construction Gains Momentum, Project Teams Are Facing New Risks and Finding Limited Solutions. *Green Source* July. Available at http://greensource.construction.com/features/other/2009/0907_Eco-design-risks.asp.

Building Operating Management. 2008. Roofing Selection Goes Life-Cycle. Report prepared for the Center for Environmental Innovation in Roofing. Available at http://www.facilitiesnet.com/roofing/article/Roofing-Selection-Goes-LifeCycle-9400.

Burr, A. 2009. Greenwashing or Just Misunderstood? Increase in Dubious Claims of LEED Certification Seen in Marketplace. Available at http://www.costar.com/News/Article.aspx?id=52FEBE64EE17E61C91E602FACB4E691C&%20ref=1&src=rss.

Cantor, S. L. 2008. *Green Roofs in Sustainable Landscape Design*. W. W. Norton & Company, New York.

Carus, F. 2009. Living Walls and Green Roofs Pave Way for Biodiversity in New Building. Available at http://www.guardian.co.uk/environment/2009/mar/30/green-building-biodiversity.

Cavanaugh, L. M. 2008. Green Roofs: The Durability-Sustainability Link. *Maintenance Solutions* August. Available at http://

www.facilitiesnet.com/roofing/article/Green-Roofs-The-DurabilitySustainability-Link-9420.

Center for Watershed Protection. 2003. Impacts of Impervious Cover on Aquatic Systems. Available at http://www.cwp.org/Resource_Library/Why_Watersheds/.

Center for Watershed Protection. 2006. Spotlight on Superior Stormwater Programs: Philadelphia. Available at *www.cwp.org/RR_Photos/philadelphiaprofile.pdf.*

Cheatham, C. 2009a. USGBC Addresses Performance Gap. Post on *Green Building Law Update* blog. Available at http://www.greenbuildinglawupdate.com/2009/07/articles/legal-developments/usgbc-addresses-performance-gap/#comments.

Cheatham, C. 2009b. The Future of LEED: Recertification. Post on *Green Building Law Update* blog. Available at http://www.greenbuildinglawupdate.com/2009/09/articles/trends/the-future-of-leed-recertification/.

City of Portland, Bureau of Environmental Services (CoPBES). 2009a. Combined Sewer Overflow Program Progress Report, January 2009. Available at http://www.portlandonline.com/cso/index.cfm?c=31727.

City of Portland, Bureau of Environmental Services (CoPBES). 2009b. News release: EPA Drops Proposed CSO Enforcement Action Against Portland. 4 March. Available at *www.portlandonline.com/shared/cfm/image.cfm?id=234472.*

City of Portland, Bureau of Environmental Services (CoPBES). *2009c. Ecoroof Handbook. Available at http://www.portlandonline.com/BES/index.cfm?c=50818&.*

Clark, C., P. Adriaens, and F. B. Talbot. 2008. Green Roof Valuation: A Probabilistic Economic Analysis of Environmental Benefits. *Environmental Science and Technology* 42(6):2155–2161.

CNA. 2009. CNA Announces EcoCare Property Upgrade Extension Endorsement. Available at http://www.cna.com/portal/site/cna/menuitem.4937ffd9e296769bc9828081a86631a0?vgnextoid=dcfd2855e0f30210VgnVCM200000751e0c0aRCRD.

Coffman, R., and T. Waite. 2009. Vegetative Roofs as Reconciled Habitats: Rapid Assays Beyond Mere Species Counts. *Urban Habitats* 6(1). Available at http://www.urbanhabitats.org/v06n01/.

Commission for Environmental Cooperation. 1997. *Ecological Regions of North America: Toward a Common Perspective.* Available at ftp://ftp.epa.gov/wed/ecoregions/na/CEC_NAeco.pdf.

Construction Specifications Institute and Construction Specifications Canada. 2008. Section Format/Page Format: The Recommended Format for Construction Specifications. Available at http://www.csinet.org/s_csi/sec.asp?TRACKID=&CID=1352&DID=11123.

Corral, O. 2009. Demand on the Rise for Green Buildings. *Miami Herald* 13 July. Available at http://www.miamiherald.com/news/southflorida/v-fullstory/story/1138219.html.

D'Annunzio, J. A. 2003. Roof System Design Standards. *Roofing Contractor* April, reprinted by *Roofing Technology*. Available at http://www.roofingtechmag.net/pages/vol4Iss1/designstandards.html.

Davis, W. N. 2009. Green Grow the Lawsuits. *ABA Journal* February. Available at http://abajournal.com/magazine/green_grow_the_lawsuits/.

Deutsch, B., H. Whitlow, M. Sullivan, A. Savineau, and B. Busiek. 2007. The Green Build-out Model: Quantifying the Stormwater Management Benefits of Trees and Green Roofs in Washington, D.C. Available at http://www.caseytrees.org/planning/greener-development/gbo/index.php.

Dunnett, N., and N. Kingsbury. 2008. *Planting Green Roofs and Living Walls*. Timber Press, Portland, Oregon.

Elvidge, C. D., C. Milesi, J. B. Dietz, B. T. Tuttle, P. C. Sutton, R. Nemani, and J. E. Vogelmann. 2004. U.S. Constructed Area Approaches the Size of Ohio. *Eos* 85(24):233–240. Available at *www.agu.org/pubs/crossref/2004/2004EO240001.shtml*.

Evans, J. 2006. Roof Inspections: A Closer Look. *Maintenance Solutions* October. Available at http://www.facilitiesnet.com/roofing/article/Roof-Inspections-A-Closer-Look-5441.

Factory Mutual Global. 2007. Property Loss Prevention Data Sheet 1-35: Green Roof Systems. Available at http://www.fmglobalcatalog.com/Default.aspx.

Forschungsgesellschaft Landschaftsentwicklung Landschaftsbau e. V. 2008. *Guideline for the Planning, Execution, and Upkeep of Green Roof Sites*. Forschungsgesellschaft Landschaftsentwicklung Landschaftsbau e. V., Bonn. Available at http://www.roofmeadow.com/technical/fll.php.

Friedrich, C. R. 2005. Principles for Selecting the Proper Components for a Green Roof Growing Media. Available at http://www.permatill.com/Greenroof_Growing_Media_Summary.pdf.

Friedrich, C. R., and S. Marlowe. 2009. Drought and the Discovery Place Green Roof Trials: A Research Project. Presentation at the Greening Rooftops for Sustainable Communities conference, Atlanta, Georgia. Available at http://guest.cvent.com/EVENTS/Info/Summary.aspx?e=65ca54a3-0023-419c-949b-d2382747e4cb.

Gangnes, D. 2007. Magnusson Klemencic Associates Update: Seattle Green Roof Evaluation Project Final Report. Available at http://www.ci.seattle.wa.us/dpd/GreenBuilding/OurProgram/Resources/TechnicalBriefs/DPDS_009485.asp.

Gedge, D. 2003. From Rubble to Redstarts. Prepared for the Greening Rooftops for Sustainable Communities conference, Chicago.

Available at http://guest.cvent.com/EVENTS/Info/Summary. aspx?e=65ca54a3-0023-419c-949b-d2382747e4cb.

Gedge, D., and G. Kadas. 2005. Green Roofs and Biodiversity. *Biologist* 52(3):161–169.

Gedge, D., and J. Little. 2008. *The DIY Guide to Green and Living Roofs*. Available at http://www.livingroofs.org/DIY_Guide_intro. html.

Getter, K. L., D. B. Rowe, and J. A. Andersen. 2007. Quantifying the Effect of Slope on Green Roof Stormwater Retention. *Ecological Engineering* 31:225–231.

Getter, K. L., D. B. Rowe, G. P. Robertson, B. M. Gregg, and J. A. Andersen. 2009. Carbon Sequestration Potential of Extensive Green Roofs. *Environmental Science and Technology* 43(19): 7170–7174.

Graham, M. 2007. Technical bulletin: NRCA's New Green Roof Systems Manual. Available at http://docserver.nrca.net/pdfs/ technical/9070.pdf.

Greer, R. K. 2008. Mimicking Pre-Development Hydrology Using LID: Time for a Reality Check? Proceedings of the International Low-Impact Development Conference, Seattle, Washington. Available at http://www.proceedings.com/05231.html.

Handwerk, B. 2004. Landscaped Roofs Have Chicago Mayor Seeing Green. *National Geographic News* 15 November. Available at http://news.nationalgeographic.com/news/2004/11/ 1115_041115_green_roofs.html.

Harrington, J. 2008. The Greening of Property Insurance. [American Association of Insurance Services] *Viewpoint* 33(1). Available at http://www.aaisonline.com/Viewpoint/2008/08sum3.html.

Harris, A. 2009. Rainwater Rules Cast Cloud over Development. Available at http://www.richmondbizsense.com/2009/07/17/ rainwater-rules-cast-cloud-over-development/.

Harris, C. M. 1988. *Time-Saver Standards for Landscape Architecture*. McGraw, New York.

Hoff, J. L. 2008. Life Cycle Assessment and the LEED Green Building Rating System. Available at http://www. roofingcenter.org/syncshow/uploaded_media/Documents/ Life%20Cycle%20Assessment%20and%20the%20LEED%20Gr een%20Building%20Rating%20System.PDF.

Johnson, M. H. 2007. Reconsidering Value Engineering. *Civil Engineer* February. Available at http://pubs.asce.org/magazines/ CEMag/2007/Issue_02-07/article1.htm.

Kamenetz, A. 2007. The Green Standard? LEED Buildings Get Lots of Buzz, But the Point Is Getting Lost. *Fast Company* October. Available at http://www.fastcompany.com/magazine/119/ the-green-standard.html?page=0%2C1.

Kauffman, T. 2009. The Re-roofing of Government. Available at http://www.federaltimes.com/index.php?S=4044663.

King, J. 2009. Letter. *Landscape Architecture* October.

King County Department of Natural Resources and Parks, Wastewater Treatment Division. 2008. Combined Sewer Overflow Control Program 2007–2008 Annual Report. Available at http://www.kingcounty.gov/environment/wastewater/CSO/Library/AnnualReports.aspx.

Klinenberg, E. 2002. *Heat Wave: A Social Autopsy of Disaster in Chicago*. University of Chicago Press, Chicago.

Köhler, M. 2003. Plant Survival Research and Biodiversity: Lessons from Europe. Presented at the Greening Rooftops for Sustainable Communities conference, Chicago. Available at http://guest.cvent.com/EVENTS/Info/Summary.aspx?e=65ca54a3-0023-419c-949b-d2382747e4cb.

Köhler, M. 2006. Long-Term Vegetation Research on Two Extensive Green Roofs in Berlin. *Urban Habitats* 4. Available at http://www.urbanhabitats.org/v04n01/berlin_full.html.

Köhler, M., and M. Schmidt. 2003. Study of Extensive Green Roofs in Berlin. Part III. Retention of Contaminants. Available at http://www.roofmeadow.com/technical/publications.php.

Kolker, K. 2008. Company Blames Rapid as Green Roof Dries Out. *The Grand Rapids Press* 29 February. Available at http://blog.mlive.com/grpress/2008/02/company_blames_rapid_a_green_r.html.

Kottek, M., J. Grieser, C. Beck, B. Rudolf, and F. Rubel. 2006. World Map of the Köppen-Geiger Climate Classification Updated. *Meteorologische Zeitschrift* 15:259–263. Available at http://koeppen-geiger.vu-wien.ac.at/.

Kurtz, T. 2008. Flow Monitoring of Three Ecoroofs in Portland, Oregon. Presented at the American Society of Civil Engineers Low-Impact Development conference, Seattle, Washington. Available at http://www.proceedings.com/05231.html.

Larsen, J. 2003. Record Heat Wave in Europe Takes 35,000 Lives: Far Greater Losses May Lie Ahead. Available at http://www.earth-policy.org/index.php?/plan_b_updates/2003/update29.

Lenart, M. 2009. Desert Prototype. *Landscape Architecture* October.

Liptan, T. 2003. Planning, Zoning, and Financial Incentives for Ecoroofs in Portland, Oregon. Prepared for the Greening Rooftops for Sustainable Communities conference, Chicago. Available at http://guest.cvent.com/EVENTS/Info/Summary.aspx?e=65ca54a3-0023-419c-949b-d2382747e4cb.

Luckett, K. 2009a. *Green Roof Construction and Maintenance*. McGraw-Hill, New York.

Luckett, K. 2009b. Green Roof Wind Uplift Challenges: Paranoia, Turn a Blind Eye, or How About We Work Together? Available at http://www.greenroofs.com/content/greenroofguy003.htm.

Lundholm, J. T. 2006. Green Roofs and Facades: A Habitat Template Approach. *Urban Habitats* 4. Available at http://www.urbanhabitats.org/v04n01/habitat_full.html.

MacMullen, E., S. Reich, T. Puttman, and K. Rodgers. 2008. Cost-Benefit Evaluation of Ecoroofs. Presented at the American Society of Civil Engineers Low-Impact Development conference, Seattle, Washington. Available at http://www.proceedings.com/05231.html.

Malin, N. 2005. Green Globes Emerges to Challenge LEED. *Environmental Building News* 14:3. Available at http://www.buildinggreen.com/auth/article.cfm?fileName=140304b.xml.

Marinelli, J. 2007. Green Roofs Take Root. *National Wildlife*, December 2007/January 2008, 46(1). Available at http://www.nwf.org/NationalWildlife/article.cfm?issueID=119&articleID=1538.

Maryland Department of the Environment. 2000. Maryland Stormwater Design Manual. Available at http://www.mde.state.md.us/Programs/WaterPrograms/SedimentandStormwater/stormwater_design/index.asp.

McCarthy, B. C. 2008. Plant Community Ecology course material. Available at http://www.plantbio.ohiou.edu/epb/instruct/commecology/ppt/LEC-1ai.pdf.

McIntyre, L. 2007a. Early Adopter. *Landscape Architecture* November.

McIntyre, L. 2007b. Grassroots Green Roof. *Landscape Architecture* December.

McIntyre, L. 2008a. State of the Art. *Landscape Architecture* June.

McIntyre, L. 2008b. A Spot of Green in Steel City. *Landscape Architecture* September.

McIntyre, L. 2009. High-Maintenance Superstar. *Landscape Architecture* August.

Miller, C. 2003. How to Assess Retention/Drainage Sheets. Available at http://www.roofmeadow.com/technical/publications.php.

Miller, C. 2008. Role of Green Roofs in Managing Thermal Energy. Available at http://www.roofmeadow.com/technical/publications.php.

Miller, C. 2009a. Roof Media Selection. Available at http://www.roofmeadow.com/technical/publications.php.

Miller, C. 2009b. Designing for the Long Term. Presentation to University of Maryland landscape architecture students. Webcast available at http://www.psla.umd.edu/PLSC/|SeminarsGreen Roof.cfm.

Miller, C., and C. Eichhorn. 2003. A New Leak Detection Technique. Available at http://www.roofmeadow.com/technical/publications.php.

Miller, N., J. Spivey, and A. Florance. 2008. Does Green Pay Off? *Journal of Sustainable Real Estate*. Available at http://www.costar.com/josre/.

Monterusso, M. A., D. B. Rowe, and C. L. Rugh. 2005. Establishment and Persistence of *Sedum* spp., and Native Taxa for Green Roof Applications. *HortScience* 40(2):391–396.

Moran, A., B. Hunt, and J. Smith. 2005. Hydrologic and Water Quality Performance from Green Roofs in Goldsboro and Raleigh, North Carolina. Available at http://www.bae.ncsu.edu/greenroofs/GRHC2005paper.pdf.

National Oceanic and Atmospheric Administration. No date. Economics of Heavy Rain and Flooding Data and Products information page. Available at http://www.economics.noaa.gov/?goal=weather&file=events/precip. Bibliography for Estimate of Economic Damage by Flooding in the U.S. in 2007. Available at http://www.ncdc.noaa.gov/oa/reports/billionz.html.

National Research Council. 2008. *Urban Stormwater Management in the United States*. The National Academies Press, Washington, D.C.

National Roofing Contractors Association (NRCA). No date. Roofing Warranties Advisory Bulletin. Available at http://www.nrca.net/consumer/warranties.aspx.

National Roofing Contractors Association (NRCA). 2009. *Vegetative Roof Systems Manual*. 2nd ed. National Roofing Contractors Association, Rosemont, Illinois.

Natural Resources Conservation Service. 2003. 2001 Annual Natural Resources Inventory: Urbanization and Development of Rural Land. Available at http://www.nrcs.usda.gov/technical/NRI/2001/nri01dev.html.

Natural Resources Defense Council. 2008. Testing the Waters: A Guide to Water Quality at Vacation Beaches. Available at http://www.nrdc.org/water/oceans/ttw/titinx.asp.

Oberdorfer, E., J. Lundholm, B. Bass, R. R. Coffman, H. Doshi, N. Dunnett, S. Gaffin, M. Köhler, K. K. Y. Liu, and B. Rowe. 2007. Green Roofs as Urban Ecosystems: Ecological Structures, Functions, and Services. *BioScience* 57(10):823–833.

Ortega-Wells, A. 2009. It's Not Easy Being Green, But It's Profitable. *Insurance Journal* April. Available at http://www.insurancejournal.com/news/ational/2009/04/21/99798.htm.

Peck, S. 2008. *Award Winning Green Roof Designs*. Shiffer Publishing Ltd., Atglen, Pennsylvania.

Penn State University, College of Agricultural Sciences, Agricultural Analytical Services Lab. No date. Green Roof Media Testing. Available at http://www.aasl.psu.edu/Greenroof.html.

Philadelphia Water Department, Office of Watersheds. 2008. City of Philadelphia Stormwater Management Guidance Manual.

Available at http://www.phillyriverinfo.org/Programs/
SubprogramMain.aspx?Id=StormwaterManual.

Philadelphia Water Department. 2009. Green City, Clean Waters:
The City of Philadelphia's Program for Combined Sewer Overflow Control: A Long-Term Control Plan Update. Available at
http://www.phillywatersheds.org/ltcpu/.

Philippi, P. 2005. Introduction to the German FLL Guideline for the
Planning, Execution, and Upkeep of Green Roof Sites. Available
at http://www.greenroofservice.com/download.html.

Philippi, P. 2006. How to Get Cost Reduction in Green Roof
Construction. Available at http://www.greenroofservice.com/
downpdf/Boston%20Paper.pdf.

Pitt, R. 1999. Small Storm Hydrology and Why It Is Important for
the Design of Stormwater Control Practices. Pp. 61–90 in *Ad-
vances in Modeling the Management of Stormwater Impacts*, Volume
7. Edited by W. James. Computational Hydraulics International,
Guelph, Ontario, and Lewis Publishers/CRC Press, Boca Raton,
Florida.

Porsche, U., and M. Köhler. 2003. Life Cycle Costs of Green Roofs:
A Comparison of Germany, USA, and Brazil. Proceedings of the
World Climate and Energy Event, Rio de Janeiro, Brazil, 1–5
December. Available at www.gruendach-mv.de/en/RIO3_461_
U_Porsche.pdf.

Posner, A. 2008. Becoming a LEED Accredited Professional. Available at http://www.treehugger.com/files/2008/08/becoming-leed-
accredited-professional.php.

Post, N. 2009. Building Rating System Requirement Raises
Concerns. *Engineering News-Record*, 8 July. Available at
http://enr.ecnext.com/comsite5/bin/comsite5.pl?page=enr_
document&item_id=0271-55750&format_id=XML.

Rana Creek. 2007. Modular Biotrays Press Release. Available at
http://www.ranacreek.com/.

Roberts, T. 2009. LEED AP Credential Program Overhauled. *Green
Source*. Available at http://greensource.construction.com/news/
2009/090126LEEDAP.asp.

Rooflite Green Roof Media. No date. Frequently Asked Questions.
Available at http://www.rooflite.us/?faq.

Roofscapes. No date. American Green Roof Standards and Testing
Methodologies. Available at http://www.roofmeadow.com/
technical/astm.php.

Rosenzweig, C., S. Gaffin, and L. Parshall, eds. 2006. Green Roofs
in the New York Metropolitan Region: Research Report. Columbia University Center for Climate Systems Research and NASA
Goddard Institute for Space Studies, New York. Available at
http://ccsr.columbia.edu/cig/greenroofs.

Schendler, A., and R. Udall. 2005. LEED Is Broken; Let's Fix It. Available at http://www.grist.org/comments/soapbox/2005/10/26/leed/index1.html.

Schneider, J. 2008. Best Intentions: A Vegetated-Roof Failure Teaches Valuable Lessons. *Eco-Structure* April.

Schneider, K. 2006. In Chicago, a Green Economy Rises. Great Lakes Bulletin News Service. Available at http://www.mlui.org/growthmanagement/fullarticle.asp?fileid=17051.

Simmons, M. T., H. C. Venhaus, and S. Windhager. 2007. Exploiting the Attributes of Regional Ecosystems for Landscape Design: The Role of Ecological Restoration in Ecological Engineering. *Ecological Engineering* 30:201–205.

Slone, D. K., and D. E. Evans. 2003. Integrating Green Roofs and Low-Impact Design into Municipal Stormwater Regulations. Presentation for the Greening Rooftops for Sustainable Communities conference, Chicago. Available at http://guest.cvent.com/EVENTS/Info/Summary.aspx?e=65ca54a3-0023-419c-949b-d2382747e4cb.

Snodgrass, E., and L. Snodgrass. 2006. *Green Roof Plants: A Resource and Planting Guide*. Timber Press, Portland, Oregon.

Stephenson, R. 1994. *Sedum: Cultivated Stonecrops*. Timber Press, Portland, Oregon.

St. John, A. 2008. Green Acres: Construction Services, a Tecta America Company, Installs a Vegetative Roof System on the Birmingham SSA Center. *Professional Roofing* December. Available at http://www.professionalroofing.net/article.aspx?id=1402.

Storm Water Infrastructure Matters (SWIM) Coalition. 2008. Press release: New York City to Clean up Waterways by Greening Roadways and Roofs. Available at http://swimmablenyc.info/.

Taylor, B. 2008. The Stormwater Control Potential of Green Roofs in Seattle. Prepared for the American Society of Civil Engineers Low-Impact Development conference, Seattle, Washington. Available at http://www.proceedings.com/05231.html.

Taylor, B., and D. Gangnes. 2004. Method for Quantifying Runoff Reduction of Green Roofs. Prepared for the Green Roofs for Healthy Cities Conference, Portland, Oregon. Available at http://guest.cvent.com/EVENTS/Info/Summary.aspx?e=65ca54a3-0023-419c-949b-d2382747e4cb.

Thomson, D. 2009. Don't Be Colorblind to Green Risks. *Construction Bulletin*. Available at http://www.acppubs.com/article/CA6655164.html.

Traver, R. G. 2009. Testimony before the U.S. House of Representatives Committee on Transportation and Infrastructure Subcommittee on Water Resources and the Environment, 19 March. Available at http://transportation.house.gov/hearings/hearingdetail.aspx?NewsID=833.

U.S. Composting Council. No date. Program information. Available at http://www.compostingcouncil.org/programs/.

U.S. Department of Agriculture. No date. Plant Hardiness Zone Map. Available at http://www.usna.usda.gov/Hardzone/ushzmap.html.

U.S. Department of Energy, Energy Information Administration. 2001. Electricity Consumption by End Use in U.S. Households. Available at http://www.eia.doe.gov/emeu/reps/enduse/er01_us_tab1.html.

U.S. Department of Energy, Energy Information Administration. 2009. *Annual Energy Outlook 2009 With Projections to 2030*. Report DOE/EIA-0383. Available at http://www.eia.doe.gov/oiaf/aeo/index.html.

U.S. Environmental Protection Agency (EPA). No date. National Pollutant Discharge Elimination System Sanitary Sewer Overflow information page. Available at http://cfpub.epa.gov/npdes/home.cfm?program_id=4.

U.S. Environmental Protection Agency (EPA). 1994. *What Is Nonpoint Source (NPS) Pollution? Questions and Answers*. Information taken from EPA Pollution Brochure EPA-841-F-94-005. Available at http://www.epa.gov/owow/nps/qa.html.

U.S. Environmental Protection Agency (EPA). 2002. Watershed Hydrology Pertinent to BMP Design. In *Considerations in the Design of Treatment Best Management Practices (BMPs) to Improve Water Quality*. EPA/600/R-03/103. National Risk Management Research Laboratory, Office of Research and Development, Cincinnati, Ohio. Available at http://www.epa.gov/ORD/NRMRL/pubs/600r03103/600r03103.htm.

U.S. Environmental Protection Agency (EPA). 2004a. *Report to Congress: Impacts and Control of CSOs and SSOs*. EPA/833/R-01/001. Available at http://cfpub.epa.gov/npdes/cso/cpolicy_report2004.cfm.

U.S. Environmental Protection Agency (EPA). 2004b. *Stormwater Best Management Practice Design Guide*. Volume 1, *General Considerations*. EPA/600/R-04/121. Office of Research and Development, Washington, D.C. Available at *www.epa.gov/nrmrl/pubs/600r04121/600r04121.pdf*.

U.S. Environmental Protection Agency (EPA). 2009a. *Green Roofs for Stormwater Runoff Control*. EPA/600/R-09/026. National Risk Management Research Laboratory, Office of Research and Development, Cincinnati, Ohio. Available at http://www.epa.gov/nrmrl/pubs/600r09026/600r09026.htm.

U.S. Environmental Protection Agency (EPA). 2009b. *Technical Guidance on Implementing Section 438 of the Energy Independence and Security Act*. Draft for discussion with the Interagency Sustainability Working Group. Available at http://www.epa.gov/owow/nps/lid/section438/.

U.S. Environmental Protection Agency (EPA). 2009c. *Managing Wet Weather with Green Infrastructure: Municipal Handbook—Incentives.* EPA/833/F-09/001. Available at http://cfpub2.epa.gov/npdes/greeninfrastructure/munichandbook.cfm.

U.S. General Services Administration. No date. Public Building Service Overview. Available at http://www.gsa.gov/Portal/gsa/ep/contentView.o?contentType=GSA_OVERVIEW&contentId=8062.

U.S. General Services Administration. 2008a. *Assessing Green Building Performance: A Post Occupancy Evaluation of 12 GSA Buildings.* PNNL-17393. GSA Public Buildings Service, Office of Applied Science, Pacific Northwest National Laboratory, Richland, Washington. Available at http://www.wbdg.org/research/sustainablehpbs.php?a=8.

U.S. General Services Administration. 2008b. *Sustainability Matters.* GSA Public Buildings Service, Office of Applied Science. Available at http://www.gsa.gov/Portal/gsa/ep/contentView.do?contentType=GSA_OVERVIEW&contentId=8154.

U.S. Geological Survey. 2008. Floods: Recurrence Intervals and 100-Year Floods. Available at http://ga.water.usgs.gov/edu/100yearflood.html.

U.S. Geological Survey. 2009. Water Properties. Available at http://ga.water.usgs.gov/edu/waterproperties.html.

U.S. Green Building Council (USGBC). No date. About USGBC: USGBC Programs. Press kit available at www.usgbc.org.

U.S. Green Building Council. 2009. LEED Initiatives in Government and Schools: Federal Initiatives. Available at http://www.usgbc.org/DisplayPage.aspx?CMSPageID=1852#federal.

Van Woert, N. D., B. Rowe, J. A. Andersen, D. L. Rugh, R. T. Fernandez, and L. Xiao. 2005. Green Roof Stormwater Retention: Effects of Roof Surface, Slope, and Media Depth. *Journal of Environmental Quality* 34:1036–1044.

Victor O. Schinnerer & Company, Inc. 2009. LEED Accredited Professionals Program Changes Risk Profiles. *Guidelines* 3-2009. Available at http://www.schinnerer.com/risk-mgmt/Gdlns/Pages/Gdlns-3-2009-pandemic-preparation.aspx.

Wanielista, M., M. Hardin, and M. Kelly. 2007. The Effectiveness of Green Roof Stormwater Treatment Systems Irrigated with Recycled Green Roof Filtrate to Achieve Pollutant Removal with Peak and Volume Reduction in Florida. Florida Department of Environmental Protection Project Number WM 864. Available at http://www.stormwater.ucf.edu/research_publications.asp#greenroof.

Wanielista, M., M. Hardin, and M. Kelly. 2008. A Comparative Analysis of Green Roof Designs Including Depth of Media,

Drainage Layer Materials, and Pollution Control Media. Florida Department of Environmental Protection Project Number WM 864. Available at http://www.stormwater.ucf.edu/research_publications.asp#greenroof.

Webber III, C. L., M. A. Harris, J. W. Shrefler, M. Durnovo, and C. A. Christopher. 2005. Organic Weed Control with Vinegar. Pp. 34–36 in *2004 Vegetable Trial Report*. MP-162. Edited by L. Brandenberger and L. Wells. Oklahoma State University, Division of Agricultural Sciences and Natural Resources, Department of Horticulture and Landscape Architecture, Stillwater. Abstract available at http://www.ars.usda.gov/research/publications/publications.htm?SEQ_NO_115=176567.

Weiler, S., and K. Scholz-Barth. 2009. *Green Roof Systems: A Guide to the Planning, Design, and Construction of Landscapes over Structure.* John Wiley & Sons, Hoboken, New Jersey.

Weinstein, N., and C. Kloss. 2009. The Implications of Section 438 for Green Technology. *Stormwater* March/April.

Weitman, D., A. Weiberg, and R. Goo. 2008. Reducing Stormwater Costs through LID Strategies and Practices. Presented at the American Society of Civil Engineers Low-Impact Development conference, Seattle, Washington. Available at http://www.proceedings.com/05231.html.

Wheeler, L., and G. Smith. 2008. Aging Systems Releasing Sewage into Rivers, Streams. *USA Today* 7 May. Available at http://www.usatoday.com/news/nation/2008-05-07-sewers-main_N.htm.

Willoughby, M. 2008. Insurers Warn of Fire Risk from Green Roofs. *Property Week* 5 September. Available at http://www.propertyweek.com/story.asp?sectioncode=29&storycode=3121655&c=1.

Wingfield, A. 2005. The Filter, Drain, and Water Holding Components of Green Roof Design. Available at http://www.greenroofs.com/archives/gf_mar05.htm.

Yocca, D. 2002. Submission for 2002 ASLA Design Awards, Chicago City Hall green roof. Available at http://www.asla.org/meetings/awards/awds02/chicagocityhall.html.

Index

Arduino®

2nd Edition

by John Nussey

A Wiley Brand

Arduino® For Dummies®, 2nd Edition

Published by: **John Wiley & Sons, Inc.**, 111 River Street, Hoboken, NJ 07030-5774, www.wiley.com

Copyright © 2018 by John Wiley & Sons, Inc., Hoboken, New Jersey

Published simultaneously in Canada

For general information on our other products and services, please contact our Customer Care Department within the U.S. at 877-762-2974, outside the U.S. at 317-572-3993, or fax 317-572-4002. For technical support, please visit https://hub.wiley.com/community/support/dummies.

Wiley publishes in a variety of print and electronic formats and by print-on-demand. Some material included with standard print versions of this book may not be included in e-books or in print-on-demand. If this book refers to media such as a CD or DVD that is not included in the version you purchased, you may download this material at http://booksupport.wiley.com. For more information about Wiley products, visit www.wiley.com.

Library of Congress Control Number: 2018951004

ISBN 978-1-119-48954-2 (pbk); ISBN 978-1-119-48955-9 (ebk); ISBN 978-1-119-48957-3 (ebk)

Manufactured in the United States of America

C10003211_080918

Arduino®

2nd Edition

by John Nussey

A Wiley Brand

Arduino® For Dummies®, 2nd Edition

Published by: **John Wiley & Sons, Inc.,** 111 River Street, Hoboken, NJ 07030-5774, www.wiley.com

Copyright © 2018 by John Wiley & Sons, Inc., Hoboken, New Jersey

Published simultaneously in Canada

For general information on our other products and services, please contact our Customer Care Department within the U.S. at 877-762-2974, outside the U.S. at 317-572-3993, or fax 317-572-4002. For technical support, please visit https://hub.wiley.com/community/support/dummies.

Wiley publishes in a variety of print and electronic formats and by print-on-demand. Some material included with standard print versions of this book may not be included in e-books or in print-on-demand. If this book refers to media such as a CD or DVD that is not included in the version you purchased, you may download this material at http://booksupport.wiley.com. For more information about Wiley products, visit www.wiley.com.

Library of Congress Control Number: 2018951004

ISBN 978-1-119-48954-2 (pbk); ISBN 978-1-119-48955-9 (ebk); ISBN 978-1-119-48957-3 (ebk)

Manufactured in the United States of America

C10003211_080918